Citrix® Access Security for IT Administrators

Citrix® Access Security for IT Administrators

CITRIX PRODUCT DEVELOPMENT TEAM

New York   Chicago   San Francisco
Lisbon   London   Madrid   Mexico City   Milan
New Delhi   San Juan   Seoul   Singapore   Sydney   Toronto

McGraw-Hill books are available at special quantity discounts to use as premiums and sales promotions, or for use in corporate training programs. For more information, please write to the Director of Special Sales, Professional Publishing, McGraw-Hill, Two Penn Plaza, New York, NY 10121-2298. Or contact your local bookstore.

Citrix® Access Security for IT Administrators

1 2 3 4 5 6 7 8 9 0   DOC DOC   0 1 9 8 7 6
ISBN-13:   978-0-07-148543-2
ISBN-10:   0-07-148543-0

Sponsoring Editor
  Wendy Rinaldi
Editorial Supervisor
  Janet Walden
Project Manager
  Patricia Wallenburg
Acquisitions Coordinator
  Mandy Canales

Copy Editor
  Eric Lowenkron
Proofreader
  Paul Tyler
Indexer
  Karin Arrigoni
Production Supervisor
  Jean Bodeaux

Technical Editor
  Kyle Randolph
Composition
  Patricia Wallenburg
Illustration
  Patricia Wallenburg
Art Director, Cover
  Jeff Weeks

AT A GLANCE

CONTENTS

FOREWORD

I n today's business environment, on-demand access to information is critical to maintaining a competitive edge. The high value of this business-critical information mandates that it must be protected. Enabling IT teams to provision enterprise resources so that end users have secure, instant access to information makes business more agile. Critical data and company assets are accessed from the Internet, airport, PDA, and cell phone, as well as the intranet. Citrix Access Security makes it possible to take advantage of a range of options for delivering integrated data security with strong countermeasures. This makes it easy to launch new applications and new services successfully, guaranteeing information system security without delaying projects, and ensures that the integration of security tools into the legacy infrastructure does not cause any drop in security or productivity.

Secure access means the data is protected and only goes where it needs to. Increased regulation worldwide, both by governments and within industries, has resulted in greater accountability for corporate officers, who now must demonstrate that they are protecting corporate information assets effectively. Stringent audit requirements have increased the need for control, visibility, and accountability. This book demonstrates how to implement the secure access functionality in Citrix products.

Citrix combines benefits that deliver a high degree of control over information and can be leveraged throughout an organization, from the data center to the endpoint, no matter what device or where. This level of control corresponds to significant compliance requirements for internal IT controls and business processes. As a result, organizations can balance information security with business productivity and cost-efficiency, optimizing controls with exceptional granularity but also great flexibility.

Each chapter of this book will help the reader understand what security features are provided by Citrix Presentation Server and Password Manager, how to use them, and what benefits they provide that help an organization build a secure access infrastructure. The threat model analysis described in each product chapter will help security professionals understand the security threats and countermeasures in a Citrix environment. The steps that follow this analysis show Citrix administrators how to implement the countermeasures in their infrastructure. Additionally, there are two chapters on secure deployments and administration. Overall, this book demonstrates the best practices for maintaining a secure access infrastructure.

Brad Pedersen
Chief Architect and Senior Fellow
Citrix Systems, Inc.

LEGAL NOTE

Please note that this volume is intended for a quick reference of the majority of Citrix products that are currently available and is not intended in any way to replace current Citrix product literature. Please visit www.citrix.com for a more comprehensive overview of the Citrix product line. In addition, while reasonable efforts have been made to ensure the accuracy and completeness of the information in this volume, products and documentation change over time. Moreover, instructions and methods applicable to your network specifications may vary from the general recommendations offered here. Users are urged to consult www.citrix.com for the most up-to-date and specific information for your specific circumstances. Finally, as users likely are aware, data security is as much an issue of legal compliance as it is a practical concern. This volume is not intended to substitute for legal advice and compliance review. Users are urged to consult with other professionals to determine whether their security practices are compliant with applicable law.

ACKNOWLEDGMENTS

Thanks to the Citrix Product Development Team—Alexander Lyublinski, Andrew Lamoureux, Anthony Ricco, Brad Pedersen, Brandon Olekas, Chris Mayers, Jennifer Lang, Kurt Roemer, Kyle Randolph, Matthew Harvey, Ola Nordstrom, Oleg Kozedub, Phil Montgomery, Tim Gaylor, Timothy Jackson—and the numerous reviewers of the draft manuscripts.

FEEDBACK ON THE GUIDE

If you have comments on this guide, send an e-mail to securitybook@citrix.com. We are particularly interested in feedback regarding the following:

▼ Technical issues specific to recommendations

■ Usefulness and usability issues

▲ Writing and editing issues

TECHNICAL SUPPORT

Technical support for the Citrix Access Suite products and technologies referenced in this guide is provided by Citrix Technical Support. For product support information, please visit the Citrix Product Support web site at http://support.citrix.com.

CHAPTER 1

Introduction

This book will give administrators a solid foundation for deploying and configuring Citrix products in a secure fashion. Whether readers are deploying their first Citrix product or have an existing Citrix deployment, they will benefit from the guidance provided in this book.

HOW TO USE THIS BOOK

The product chapters in this book can be read in any order. All of those chapters have the same structure. The first section of each chapter provides a threat model of the specified Citrix product or component, and the second section provides step-by-step instructions for implementing countermeasures to those threats.

Depending on your security goals, you will be interested in different portions of the book. All information technology (IT) administrators who work on the design, deployment, or configuration of Citrix environments should read this chapter and Chapters 2 and 3, which deal with assets, threats, countermeasures, security fundamentals, and administrative best practices.

If you are responsible for the design and deployment of a Citrix environment that contains multiple products, you should begin with Chapter 2, "Secure Deployments," to determine which deployment best meets your needs. Then you can reference the individual chapters that pertain to the products you plan to use in the deployment.

If you are responsible for network setup and maintenance for an organization, your first step should be to determine which Citrix products will be deployed on the network. Armed with this information, reference the beginning of each product chapter to look at detailed diagrams that contain all the port and protocol information you will need to configure the network firewalls. You also will want to read the first section of each chapter to identify any threats that could be mitigated.

If you are responsible for the installation and administration of Citrix software, you should read all the chapters pertaining to the Citrix products you will be installing and maintaining. The first section of each chapter will help you perform a security analysis and decide which threats will require countermeasures in your environment. The second section will outline the steps required to implement those countermeasures and the means to verify that the steps were taken correctly.

THREAT MODELING

The first section of each product chapter divides a specific Citrix product into components, identifies the assets of those components, and describes the threats to those assets along with a description of potential countermeasures for those threats. The potential threats identified in this section may not be considered threats by every organization. An organization's security policy will determine which threats require countermeasures. The second section of each product chapter contains specific steps that administrators can follow to implement each countermeasure. On the basis of the threats and counter-

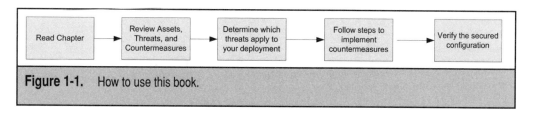

Figure 1-1. How to use this book.

measures administrators identify for their organization, they will know which steps to take and which ones are unnecessary. The steps to threat model a deployment using this book are outlined in Figure 1-1.

Components

To understand how to secure any system, one must understand the system architecture. The first step in this process is decomposing the system into individual components. A *component* is an individual piece of a product that is self-contained and can communicate with other components. Some components are optional, and some are required for a product to function.

Consider a castle, for example. A medieval castle was composed of walls, turrets, a moat, an armory, a barracks, living quarters for the owner, and a dungeon for those who misbehaved. To enter the castle, a visitor had to cross the moat. Once inside, the visitor followed streets and paths to each area of the castle. Each path served a specific purpose and allowed people to flow between the castle's components. All the buildings were components of the castle, and each had specific assets that had to be maintained or protected. The roads and paths can be thought of as the paths of communication between components.

Assets

An *asset* is an item of value that is owned by an entity. Many assets are intangible and difficult to identify. In the context of computer security, assets consist of the typical hardware, software, and data of a system. Data assets can reside in memory, in a database, or in a network cable on its way to a server.

To return to the castle example, each component of the castle has assets. The bricks in the wall must be maintained to keep the perimeter secured, the weapons in the armory must be protected and maintained, and the owner in the living quarters must be protected from everyone who does not have permission to meet with him or her. All those assets must be protected in different ways for the castle to function correctly and efficiently.

Administrators must secure two types of assets in their systems: assets associated with user data and the assets of the system itself. User data assets are present in a system before the deployment of any Citrix software. These assets can include sensitive documents, intellectual property, and customer contact sheets. Assets associated with the system are assets of the software installed on the computer. Those assets can include encryption keys, digital certificates, and registry entries. Installing a Citrix product introduces additional "Citrix assets" that an administrator must secure. A *Citrix asset* is an asset that is specific to Citrix software and is not present before installation. The product chapters in this book tell administrators about many additional system assets that they may or may not have considered. Administrators are responsible for determining which of those assets are important to the organization.

SECURITY CHARACTERISTICS

All assets have security characteristics that administrators must take into account when securing their systems. In the case of the castle, the characteristic of the bricks in the castle wall that must be protected is structural integrity, the characteristic of the weapons in the armory that must be protected is confidentiality and integrity, and the characteristic of the owners that must be protected is their physical well-being. Each asset has different characteristics, and it would not be logical to protect every asset in the same way. For example, the bricks in the castle do not have to be protected from unauthorized visitors and the owner of the castle does not have to be protected against erosion. Only by identifying the security characteristics of each asset can an administrator determine all the threats to an asset.

This book considers four general security characteristics of assets: *confidentiality, integrity, availability,* and *auditability*. This list is not comprehensive but is sufficient for the purposes of this book.

Confidentiality

The *confidentiality* of an asset refers to the fact that only authorized users are able to read, view, or print an asset or sometimes even know that it exists. A violation of confidentiality could consist of a competitor stealing intellectual property, an attacker stealing financial account information, or an attacker stealing medical records. There are several approaches to protecting the confidentiality of assets. Access to information can be physically restricted, the data can be encrypted, or access to the data could be restricted through the use of an access control list (ACL). Encryption can be used to provide confidentiality by ensuring that only a user with the correct key can view an asset. Secure Sockets Layer (SSL) is a network security technology that provides both authentication and data encryption. ACLs also can be utilized to prevent unauthorized access to data. Steps for securing the confidentiality of Citrix assets are explained in each of the product chapters.

Integrity

Data *integrity* provides protective mechanisms against unauthorized modification or destruction of information. A violation of integrity could consist of the defacement of a company website, an attacker reducing the prices of items in an online store, or even an attacker modifying user passwords to gain privileges on company machines. Administrators can protect the integrity of data both by denying access to the data and by cryptographically verifying that the data are unchanged. Some examples of security technologies that protect the integrity of data are ACLs, digital signatures, message authentication codes, and Internet Protocol Security (IPsec). Administrators should take the proper steps to configure Citrix software to protect the integrity of both Citrix assets and user data, as described in the product chapters.

Availability

The characteristic of *availability* applies to both data and services. A data asset can be considered available if it is present in a usable form, if it has sufficient capacity to respond to requests, and if a request is completed in an acceptable time period. In many organizations, system downtime leads to substantial financial losses. Systems that are unresponsive can result in lost worker productivity, lost revenue from Web sales, and loss of reputation. Availability in a Citrix environment can refer to the ability of an end user to access an application on the Citrix Presentation Server, the availability of licenses on the Citrix License Server, and the ability to access secondary credentials on the Citrix Password Manager. This book does not focus on availability. For information on creating available configurations for Citrix products, refer to the current Citrix *Advanced Concepts Guide*.

Auditability

Auditing is any action or process that is used to create and maintain a record of users' activities. This could include which users accessed a specific system and what actions they performed. Logging these events helps security personnel and administrators determine whether the security of a system has been compromised. It also aids them in determining what actions an attacker has performed on a compromised system. Citrix products offer logging features that track users' actions throughout the system. These logs can be used later to confirm or refute users' claims that they have performed a specific action on the system.

THREATS

A *threat* is a set of circumstances that has the potential to affect one or more security characteristics of an asset. After one had determined all the assets in a system and the security characteristics of each of those assets, the next step in understanding how to secure a system is identifying the threats to each asset. Threat agents (causes of threats) include people, programs, and phenomena. People can be attackers or legitimate users who perform actions accidentally. Programs can include a malicious program that is designed to attack systems or a weakness in a protocol that allows specific attacks. Phenomena are elements beyond the control of administrators, such as a power outage.

Returning to the castle example, consider the weapons in the armory. The security characteristics of those weapons are confidentiality and usability. In a privately owned castle without guards, there may be no weapons or the weapons may be only for show. In this case, there is no need to secure the weapons from unauthorized parties or keep them sharp. In castles with one or more guards, the security and usability of the weapons are important. What are the potential threats to the usability of the weapons? Those threats could include theft, vandalism, and even rust. Although none of these threats can be eliminated completely, all of them can be mitigated through the implementation of countermeasures.

Threats to a digital environment are much less tangible than are those to a castle, but the principle is the same. Each asset has a specific list of threats that endanger a security characteristic of that asset. For example, if the asset is user passwords and the security characteristics of the asset are confidentiality and integrity, what are the threats to those characteristics? Threats against confidentiality could include gaining unauthorized access to the password database, sniffing passwords on the network, and tricking users into disclosing their passwords. Threats against integrity could be unauthorized modification to the passwords in the database and the interception and modification of passwords on the network. The threats defined in each product chapter are not comprehensive, and threats vary from organization to organization. Using the information in the first section of the chapter, administrators should analyze the risk presented by each threat and decide which threats should be addressed. Each threat must be dealt with individually by choosing to accept the threat, transfer the threat, avoid and/or eliminate the threat, or mitigate the threat by implementing countermeasures. If administrators can eliminate a threat, that means they are able to remove the threat entirely. Unfortunately, some threats cannot be eliminated completely from any system because of cost, usability, or circumstances beyond

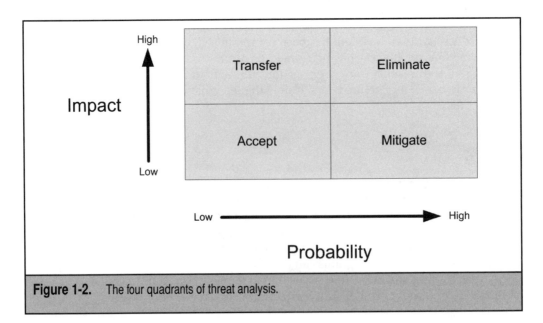

Figure 1-2. The four quadrants of threat analysis.

the administrators' control. When elimination is not an option; an administrator must try to mitigate the threat. Mitigation means alleviating risk to an acceptable extent. This four quadrant model for threat analysis can be found in Figure 1-2.

COUNTERMEASURES

Once all threats to the individual assets of each component are identified and the threats that can be eliminated or mitigated have been listed, administrators must determine which countermeasures they plan to implement.

For example, some threats to the confidentiality and usability of the weapons in the armory are theft, vandalism, and rust. In a castle that is used only as a residence, an owner may decide to accept the threat of rust because the weapons are not used. The owner also could eliminate all the threats by removing the weapons from his or her home. In a castle with guards, the options of accepting rust and removing the weapons would not be acceptable; in fact, they would reduce security. In a guarded castle, the owner could mitigate the threats of theft and vandalism by installing locks on the armory door. To add more security, the owner could have a guard stand watch at the door. To mitigate the threat of rust, weapons could be polished weekly.

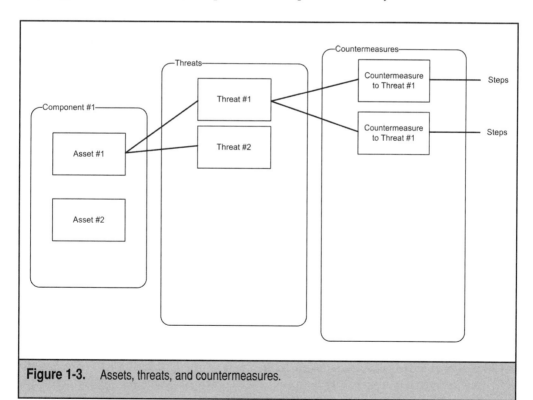

Figure 1-3. Assets, threats, and countermeasures.

A list of potential countermeasures that administrators can use to eliminate or mitigate the threats to each of the assets in their Citrix products is presented in this book. This list is not comprehensive, and administrators can choose to use countermeasures other than those presented here. Steps to implement the list of countermeasures are defined immediately after the countermeasures section. The relationship between assets, threats, countermeasures, and steps can be seen in Figure 1-3.

SECURITY TECHNOLOGIES

This book uses many security-related terms that are required to explain the assets, threats, and countermeasures in a Citrix environment. To help the reader understand the technologies described in this book, a brief discussion of security technologies follows.

Cryptography

Cryptography is the art and science of keeping information secure. Citrix uses cryptography to provide encryption, data integrity, and authentication services for its products.

Encryption is the process by which data are disguised in a way that hides their substance to all but authorized users. Citrix uses encryption to protect the confidentiality of data from attackers when the software must send data across the network and store information in databases.

Another use of cryptography is to protect the integrity of data. Information transmitted over a network is easy to intercept and modify. Cryptographic data integrity validation allows the receiver of data to verify that the data have not been modified in transit. Furthermore, data integrity validation prevents an attacker from fabricating false data. Digital signatures are a security technology that enables this protection. Citrix products use cryptography to digitally sign information to mitigate the threat of tampering.

Finally, cryptography allows for authentication. *Authentication* is the ability of a user, process, or machine to prove its identity to another entity. A program or operating system can use the identity of the authenticated entity to allow or deny access to data by using an ACL. Citrix products support several different methods of authentication. Consult Chapter 2, "Secure Deployments," for a list of authentication mechanisms for each product.

Digital Certificates

Some cryptographic keys are stored in the form of digital certificates. A *digital certificate* is a file issued to a user or machine that associates that specific entity with a unique cryptographic key. The certificate is digitally signed by a root certificate that belongs to a trusted authority. The trusted authority not only vouches for the validity of the certificates it has signed but also maintains a certificate revocation list (CRL). A CRL is a list of certificates that are invalid. Each time a certificate is verified, in addition to checking the signature and expiration date, the computer checks the CRL to ensure that the certificate has not been revoked. In this case, much in the same way a stolen credit card is canceled, a stolen certificate can be invalidated. These certificates are installed into the Microsoft certificate store and are secured by Windows.

Auditing

Auditing is the review of statistics and logs to determine information about a system. Citrix components have logging features that aid administrators in auditing. Administrators should configure their Citrix products to enable all logging features to facilitate this process. Logging gives administrators an advantage so that when there is an attempted attack, they can examine those logs to determine the source and target of the attack as well as the identity of the attacker. Not only is auditing useful in analyzing the source and result of an attack, it serves as a deterrent to attacks. If attackers know that administrators review logs and that there are penalties for violating security policies on a system, they will be less motivated to attack that system because of the potential consequences.

SUMMARY

To secure a system, administrators must understand the threat model for that system. The information in this book provides the basis for that understanding. Armed with this knowledge, administrators can make informed decisions about what assets must be protected on their systems, what the security characteristics of those assets are, and the threats to those characteristics that are present in the system. Once administrators have analyzed the threat model, they can choose countermeasures for each threat and take steps to eliminate or mitigate those threats.

CHAPTER 2

Secure Deployments

This chapter discusses the network security features of Citrix products that are available in various deployments of those products. Individuals who are responsible for selecting a deployment for Citrix products should base the choice of a deployment on the needs of the organization.

To assist those individuals in choosing an appropriate deployment, this chapter discusses three elements:

▼   Authentication mechanisms

■   Secure communications

▲   Secure deployments

Because not all authentication mechanisms and secure communication protocols are available with all network topologies, different combinations of these elements dictate certain deployment scenarios. Individuals who are responsible for designing a deployment of Citrix products should consider all requirements for authentication mechanisms, secure communications, and network topology. The remainder of this chapter discusses authentication mechanisms, secure communication protocols, and when they are supported with various network topologies.

AUTHENTICATION

Authentication refers to the ability of a user, process, or machine to prove its identity. In a Citrix environment, users authenticate to a machine by using passwords, smart cards, or similar mechanisms. Some examples of common authentication mechanisms include the following:

▼   Password

■   Smart card

■   Token

▲   Biometric

NOTE   Some of these authentication mechanisms require additional technology that must be acquired from third-party vendors.

Examples of common authentication protocols include

▼   Windows NT LAN Manager (NTLM)

▲   Kerberos

Each authentication mechanism has advantages and drawbacks. Individuals who are responsible for designing a Citrix deployment should determine which authentication mechanisms are needed in the deployment. There is a discussion of various deployment scenarios and the supported authentication mechanisms later in this chapter.

Password

The most common way to authenticate is with a *password*. This method of authentication is simple, well known, and widely available. Potential drawbacks are that passwords may be easy to guess, reused in multiple places, forgotten, or written down where others can find them, thus reducing the security of the system.

Smart Card

Smart cards are tamper-resistant devices of about credit card size, usually containing a microprocessor, that offer various security services. Citrix products use the authentication and encryption features of smart cards. Smart cards may be used for two-factor authentication. The drawback of smart cards is that they may require specialized hardware that is not present on all machines.

NOTE   Smart cards are provided by third-party vendors and must have explicit support from Citrix or the vendor to function in a Citrix environment. Some smart card solutions may have additional third-party requirements or not be supported by the third party in the deployment scenarios shown in this chapter. Before choosing a deployment, organizations that are using smart card solutions should consult the vendor.

Token

Tokens are devices that contain secret data used in authentication and may be physical or virtual. The data may be biometric data, a one-time password, digital certificates, or cryptographic keys. Such systems may be more secure than passwords alone, but have the drawback that tokens must be distributed to each user.

NOTE   Tokens are provided by third-party vendors and must have explicit support from Citrix or the vendor to function in a Citrix environment. Some token solutions may have additional third-party requirements or not be supported by the third party in the deployment scenarios shown in this chapter. Before choosing a deployment, organizations using token solutions should consult the vendor.

Biometric

Biometric authentication uses unique characteristics such as fingerprints, handprints, or retinal scans or behaviors such as typing patterns to recognize users. These systems have the advantage of not requiring an individual to remember a password or carry anything but may require special hardware.

Authentication Protocols

Windows NT LAN Manager (NTLM)

NTLM, the Windows NT LAN Manager challenge-response protocol, is a network-based authentication protocol. It is built into Windows and is the default method of authentication between Windows hosts on a network. This protocol allows users to authenticate to a remote machine. NTLM may be used to authenticate directly between two hosts or with a domain controller as a trusted authority.

The original NTLM protocol operated over the Server Message Block (SMB) protocol. Citrix products that support NTLM for authentication use a more recent standard that tunnels NTLM authentication over the Hypertext Transfer Protocol (HTTP).

Kerberos

Kerberos is another network-based authentication protocol. Kerberos uses a central Key Distribution Center (KDC) to grant tickets to access resources such as servers or printers to authorized clients. Kerberos supports cross-domain authentication and delegation, which are not supported by NTLM; however, Kerberos requires a KDC, and clients must have network access to the KDC. Windows 2000 Server and Windows Server 2003, when configured as a domain controller, include KDC functionality.

Originally, Kerberos was an independent protocol. More recently, a standard for tunneling Kerberos over HTTP was created. Citrix products that support Kerberos may use it over HTTP. Administrators should note that for Citrix products to use Kerberos, the administrators must configure the hosts to use it.

SECURE COMMUNICATIONS

Communication between Citrix products should be authenticated and have integrity protection. One way to secure communications is to use an encryption technology such as SSL, Transport Layer Security (TLS), or IPsec. In some deployments, these secure communications technologies augment the security of Citrix products. In other deployments, secure communication is required for Citrix products to function. For example, an administrator may add extra protection to Independent Management Architecture (IMA) traffic in a Citrix Presentation Server farm by using IPsec, whereas SSL/TLS is required for communication between a user and a Secure Gateway. A discussion later in this chapter shows which secure protocols are available in different deployments.

SSL/TLS

SSL and TLS are standard protocols for secure communication. These protocols may use certificates to authenticate the involved parties and negotiate the session keys that are used to encrypt traffic between the parties. SSL/TLS also can use client certificates for mutual authentication. SSL/TLS can encapsulate and encrypt traffic from other protocols, such as HTTP, and protect them against disclosure or tampering.

HTTPS

The use of HTTP Secure (HTTPS) indicates that SSL/TLS is used to encrypt HTTP traffic.

IPsec

IPsec is a protocol for encrypting and/or authenticating Internet Protocol (IP) packets. IPsec has two modes: tunnel mode and transport mode. This book discusses only the transport mode, which offers end-to-end security for all IP traffic sent between two hosts. Like SSL/TLS, IPsec requires that each endpoint have an encryption key, which is used to establish an encrypted tunnel. IPsec should be used when other secure communication protocols are not available.

SECURE DEPLOYMENTS

A *secure deployment* is one in which the threats to an organization's assets have been mitigated, eliminated, transferred, or accepted and all the organization's security policies have been followed. Citrix products can be deployed in several configurations to fit an organization's needs. The individuals responsible for designing the Citrix deployment should work with the individuals responsible for the network topology to choose a deployment that best suits the organization's needs. Items to consider include the following:

▼ Organizational policies such as the following:
  ■ All traffic between remote clients and Presentation Servers must be encrypted.
  ■ Two-factor authentication for all remote logins.
  ■ Restrictions on which software may be deployed in the DMZ.
  ■ Requirements for end-to-end encryption.
■ Deployed solutions such as the following:
  ■ Virtual Private Networks (VPNs).
  ■ Authentication mechanisms such as smart cards or tokens.
  ■ Load balancers.
  ■ Firewalls.
■ Current network topology such as the following:
  ■ Intranets.
  ■ Demilitarized zones (DMZs).
  ■ Virtual local area networks (VLANs).

- Goals of deploying Citrix products, such as the following:
  - Provide reliable access to published applications from remote locations.
  - Hide IP addresses of Presentation Servers from remote users.
  - Allow all users to authenticate by using Kerberos.
- ▲ Any other factors that affect which Citrix products can be deployed and how they will interact.

The following sections discuss common deployment scenarios. No single scenario will fit all organizations, and some organizations may choose to utilize a deployment that is not shown here. Each scenario illustrates different combinations of authentication mechanisms and secure communication protocols that are available in various deployments. After choosing a deployment, administrators should follow the steps for securing each product that are described in the corresponding product chapter.

Password Manager

Administrators can deploy the Password Manager in several ways. In a Presentation Server environment, the Password Manager Agent may be deployed as a hosted application in conjunction with a published application, as is shown in the following deployments. The Password Manager uses a central store that is either a New Technology File System (NTFS) network share or an active directory container. In these deployments, the central store and the Password Manager Service are isolated behind firewalls for protection.

Citrix License Server

Many Citrix components, including the Password Manager Agent, must have access to the Citrix License Server. To protect the license server, administrators should isolate it behind a firewall, as is shown in the following deployments.

NOTE These deployments show the license server protected by a firewall, but with a range of ports open. Administrators should consult Chapter 9, "License Server," for information on limiting this range.

Web Interface in a DMZ with Secure Gateway for Windows Deployment

The deployment shown in Figure 2-1 exposes the Web Interface and the Secure Gateway to the Internet and isolates them within a single DMZ with two firewalls, allowing clients on the Internet to connect to the Presentation Server. The Secure Gateway and the Web Interface are shown on separate hosts. It is possible but not recommended to install them on a single host. At least one host must be dedicated to the Presentation Server and the Citrix Password Manager Agent in this deployment. The Password Manager central store may reside either on a dedicated file server or on a domain controller. The Password

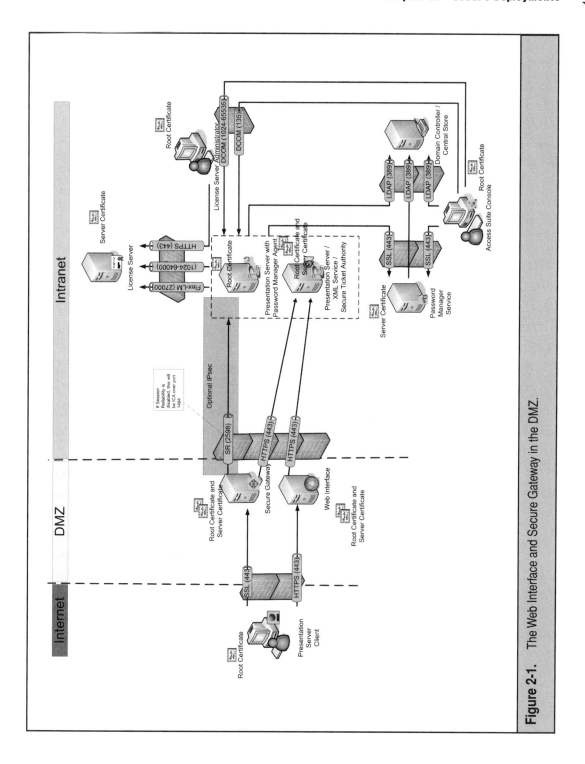

Figure 2-1.   The Web Interface and Secure Gateway in the DMZ.

Manager Service should be installed on a dedicated host. Firewalls should protect both the central store and the Password Manager Service. Here, the license server is shown on a dedicated host. It is possible to use a Presentation Server as the license server, but this increases the load on the server and eliminates the ability of administrators to protect the license server with a separate firewall.

The secure protocols in Table 2-1 are supported.

NOTE IPsec may be available in more cases than are shown here. IPsec is marked only when other secure protocols are not available.

The authentication mechanisms listed in Table 2-2 are supported.

Connection	SSL/TLS	HTTPS	IPsec
Client→Secure Gateway	✔		
Client→Web Interface		✔	
Secure Gateway→Secure Ticket Authority		✔	
Web Interface→Secure Ticket Authority		✔	
Secure Gateway→Presentation Server			✔
Web Interface→Presentation Server		✔	
Password Manager Agent→Central Store			✔
Password Manager Agent→Password Manager Service		✔	
Presentation Server→Citrix License Server			✔
Password Manager Agent→Citrix License Server			✔
Access Suite Console→Presentation Server			✔
Access Suite Console→Password Manager Service	✔		
Access Suite Console→Central Store			✔
License Management Console→License Server		✔	

Table 2-1. Secure Communication Protocols

Connection	Password	NTLM	Kerberos	Token
Client→Web Interface	✔			✔
Password Manager Agent→Central Store		✔	✔	
Access Suite Console→Presentation Server		✔		
Access Suite Console→Password Manager Service		✔		
Access Suite Console→Central Store		✔		
License Management Console→License Server		✔		

Table 2-2. Authentication Mechanisms

Secure Gateway in Front of Web Interface in a Single DMZ

The deployment shown in Figure 2-2 exposes the Secure Gateway to the Internet, allowing clients on the Internet to connect to the Presentation Server and isolating the Secure Gateway and the Web Interface within a single DMZ with two firewalls. The Secure Gateway and the Web Interface are shown on separate hosts. It is possible but not recommended to install them on a single host. At least one host must be dedicated to the Presentation Server and Password Manager Agent in this deployment. The Password Manager central store may reside either on a dedicated file server or on a domain controller. The Password Manager Service should be installed on a dedicated host. Firewalls should protect both the central store and the Password Manager Service. The license server is shown on a dedicated host. It is possible to use a Presentation Server as the license server, but this increases the load on the server and eliminates the ability of administrators to protect the license server with a separate firewall.

Administrators who use a single DMZ and do not want to expose the Web Interface to the Internet may choose this deployment. Administrators who use this deployment should note that not all of the Web Interface's features, particularly authentication mechanisms, are available in this deployment. The secure communication protocols in Table 2-3 are supported in this deployment.

NOTE IPsec may be available in more cases than are shown here. IPsec is marked when other secure protocols are not available.

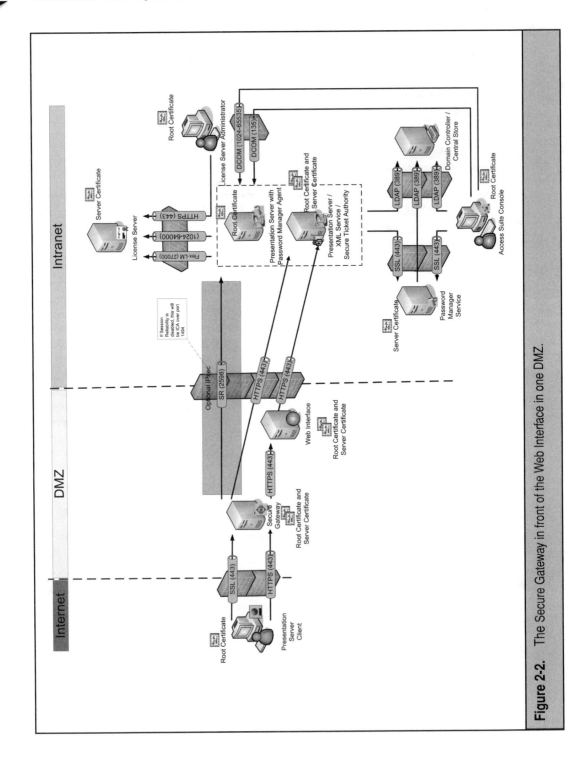

Figure 2-2. The Secure Gateway in front of the Web Interface in one DMZ.

Connection	SSL/TLS	HTTPS	IPsec
Client→Secure Gateway	✔		
Client→Web Interface		✔	
Secure Gateway→Secure Ticket Authority		✔	
Web Interface→Secure Ticket Authority		✔	
Secure Gateway→Presentation Server			✔
Web Interface→Presentation Server		✔	
Password Manager Agent→Central Store			✔
Password Manager Agent→Password Manager Service		✔	
Presentation Server→Citrix License Server			✔
Password Manager Agent→Citrix License Server			✔
Access Suite Console→Presentation Server			✔
Access Suite Console→Password Manager Service	✔		
Access Suite Console→Central Store			✔
License Management Console→License Server		✔	

Table 2-3.   Secure Communication Protocols

The authentication mechanisms listed in Table 2-4 are supported:

Connection	Password	NTLM	Kerberos
Client→Web Interface	✔		
Password Manager Agent→Central Store		✔	✔
Access Suite Console→Presentation Server		✔	
Access Suite Console→Password Manager Service		✔	
Access Suite Console→Central Store		✔	
License Management Console→License Server		✔	

Table 2-4.   Authentication Mechanisms

Web Interface, Secure Gateway, and Secure Gateway Proxy in Two DMZs

The deployment shown in Figure 2-3 utilizes two DMZs and exposes only the Secure Gateway to the Internet. This allows clients on the Internet to connect to the Presentation Server and isolates the Secure Gateway, the Secure Gateway Proxy, and the Web Interface within two DMZs with three firewalls. Administrators who choose not to expose the Web Interface directly to the Internet or who have two DMZs may find this deployment appropriate. The Secure Gateway Proxy functions as a relay in this deployment, allowing communication from the Secure Gateway to pass through the second DMZ without the need to allow traffic from the Secure Gateway to pass directly through two firewalls. In this deployment, several authentication mechanisms are unavailable.

In this deployment, the Secure Gateway and the Web Interface are on separate hosts. A host must be dedicated to the Secure Gateway Proxy. At least one host must be dedicated to the Presentation Server and Password Manager Agent in this deployment. The Password Manager central store may reside either on a dedicated file server or on a domain controller. The Password Manager Service should be installed on a dedicated host. Firewalls should protect both the central store and the Password Manager Service. The license server is shown on a dedicated host in this case. It is possible to use a Presentation Server as the license server, but this increases the load on the server and eliminates the ability of administrators to protect the license server with a separate firewall.

The secure communication protocols in Table 2-5 are supported in this deployment. The authentication mechanisms listed in Table 2-6 are supported.

Connection	SSL/TLS	HTTPS	IPsec
Client→Secure Gateway	✔	✔	
Secure Gateway→Web Interface		✔	
Secure Gateway Proxy→Secure Ticket Authority		✔	
Web Interface→Secure Ticket Authority		✔	
Secure Gateway→Secure Gateway Proxy	✔		
Secure Gateway Proxy→Presentation Server			✔
Web Interface→Presentation Server		✔	
Password Manager Agent→Central Store			✔
Password Manager Agent→Password Manager Service		✔	
Presentation Server→Citrix License Server			✔
Password Manager Agent→Citrix License Server			✔
Access Suite Console→Presentation Server			✔
Access Suite Console→Password Manager Service	✔		
Access Suite Console→Central Store			✔
License Management Console→License Server		✔	

Table 2-5.   Secure Communication Protocols

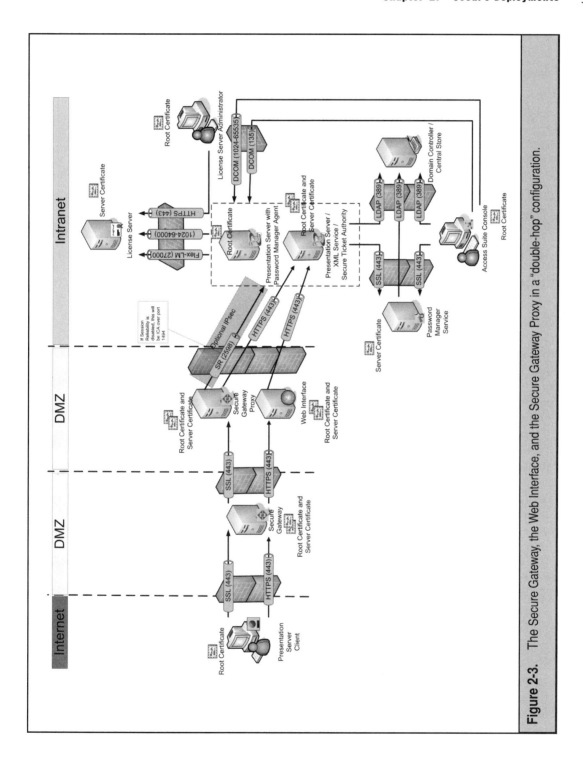

Figure 2-3. The Secure Gateway, the Web Interface, and the Secure Gateway Proxy in a "double-hop" configuration.

Connection	Password	NTLM	Kerberos
Client→Web Interface	✔		
Password Manager Agent→Central Store		✔	✔
Access Suite Console→Presentation Server		✔	
Access Suite Console→Password Manager Service		✔	
Access Suite Console→Central Store		✔	
License Management Console→License Server		✔	

Table 2-6.   Authentication Mechanisms

Web Interface in DMZ with SSL Relay

The deployment shown in Figure 2-4 exposes the Web Interface to the Internet, allowing clients on the Internet to connect to the Presentation Server and isolating the Web Interface within a single DMZ with two firewalls. Administrators who choose not to deploy the Secure Gateway but want to keep their Presentation Servers on an intranet may find this deployment convenient. This deployment allows all, even unauthenticated, Independent Computing Architecture (ICA) traffic to pass through both DMZ firewalls to the Presentation Servers.

In this deployment, the Web Interface should be installed on a dedicated host and at least one host must be dedicated to the Presentation Server and Password Manager Agent. The Password Manager central store may reside either on a dedicated file server or on a domain controller. The Password Manager Service should be installed on a dedicated host. Firewalls should protect both the central store and the Password Manager Service. In this case, the license server is shown on a dedicated host. It is possible to use a Presentation Server as the license server, but this increases the load on the server and eliminates the ability of administrators to protect the license server with a separate firewall.

The secure communication protocols in Table 2-7 are supported in this deployment.

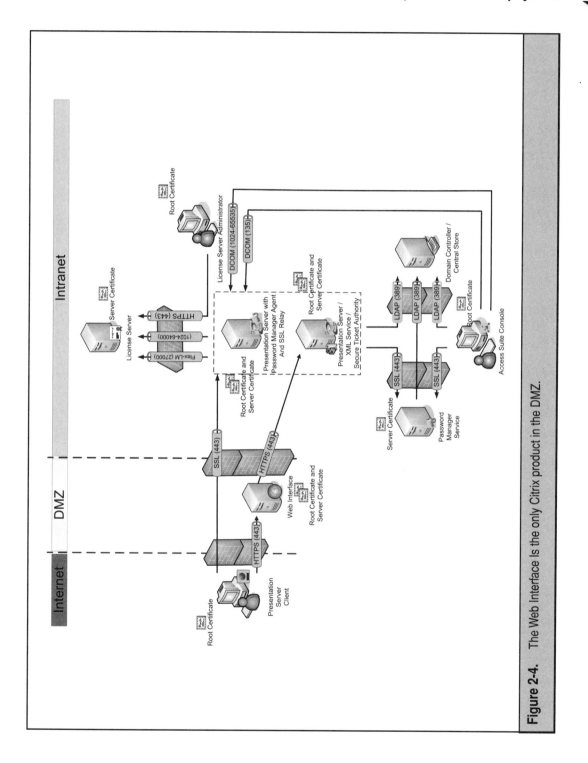

Figure 2-4.   The Web Interface Is the only Citrix product in the DMZ.

Connection	SSL/TLS	HTTPS	IPsec
Client→Web Interface		✔	
Web Interface→Secure Ticket Authority		✔	
Web Interface→Presentation Server		✔	
Password Manager Agent→Central Store			✔
Password Manager Agent→Password Manager Service		✔	
Presentation Server→Citrix License Server			✔
Password Manager Agent→Citrix License Server			✔
Access Suite Console→Presentation Server			✔
Access Suite Console→Password Manager Service	✔		
Access Suite Console→Central Store			✔
License Management Console→License Server		✔	

Table 2-7. Secure Communication Protocols

The authentication mechanisms listed in Table 2-8 are supported.

Connection	Password	NTLM	Kerberos	Token
Client→Web Interface	✔	✔		✔
Password Manager Agent→Central Store		✔	✔	
Access Suite Console→Presentation Server	✔			
Access Suite Console→Password Manager Service	✔			
Access Suite Console→Central Store	✔			
License Management Console→License Server	✔			

Table 2-8. Authentication Mechanisms

Intranet Deployment

The deployment shown in Figure 2-5 isolates all deployed Citrix products from the Internet, allowing only clients on the intranet to connect to the Presentation Server. At least one host must be dedicated to the Presentation Server in this deployment. The Password Manager Agent is deployed on the workstations, but it also can be deployed in conjunction with a published application. The Password Manager central store may reside either on a dedicated file server or on a domain controller. The Password Manager Service should be installed on a dedicated host. Firewalls should protect both the central store and the Password Manager Service. In this case, the license server is shown on a dedicated host. It is possible to use a Presentation Server as the license server, but this increases the load on the server and eliminates the ability of administrators to protect the license server with a separate firewall.

The secure communication protocols in Table 2-9 are supported in this deployment. The authentication mechanisms listed in Table 2-10 are supported.

NOTE IPsec may be available in more cases than are shown here. IPsec is marked when other secure protocols are not available.

Connection	SSL/TLS	HTTPS	IPsec
Client→Presentation Server	✔		
Password Manager Agent→Central Store			✔
Password Manager Agent→Password Manager Service		✔	
Presentation Server→Citrix License Server			✔
Password Manager Agent→Citrix License Server			✔
Access Suite Console→Presentation Server			✔
Access Suite Console→Password Manager Service	✔		
Access Suite Console→Central Store			✔
License Management Console→License Server		✔	

Table 2-9. Secure Communication Protocols

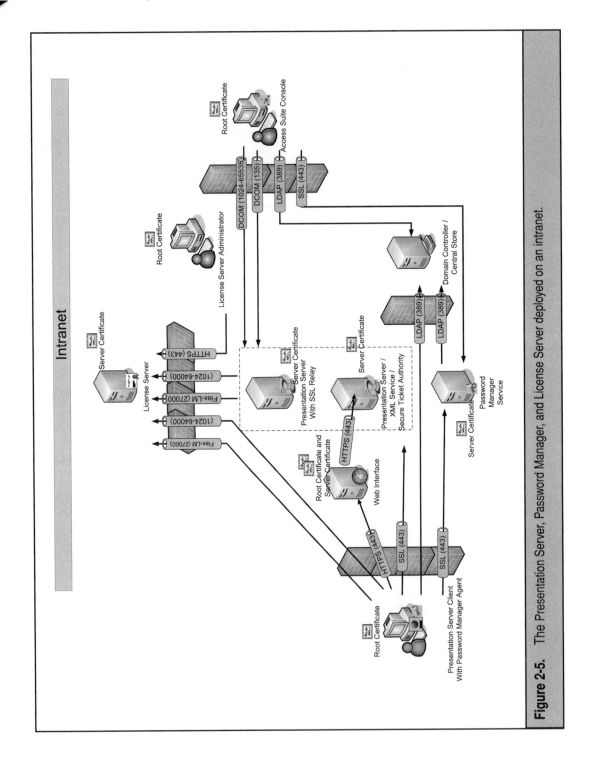

Figure 2-5. The Presentation Server, Password Manager, and License Server deployed on an intranet.

Connection	Password	NTLM	Kerberos	Smart Card	Biometric	Token
Client→Presentation Server	✔	✔	✔	✔	✔	✔
Password Manager Agent→ Central Store		✔	✔			
Access Suite Console→ Presentation Server		✔				
Access Suite Console→ Password Manager Service		✔				
Access Suite Console→Central Store		✔				
License Management Console→ License Server		✔				

Table 2-10.   Authentication Mechanisms

SUMMARY

This chapter discussed several deployments of Citrix products. Administrators should be familiar with the overall structure of a Citrix deployment and understand how the components interact. The deployment that best meets the needs of the organization should be utilized. To help administrators secure their Citrix deployments, the following chapters discuss individual products in more detail.

CHAPTER 3

Administrative Best Practices

Administrators must maintain good organizational security practices to ensure the security of their sensitive data. This chapter focuses on the best practices most relevant to the Citrix products presented in this book. Three categories of administrative practices are important to maintaining the security of a Citrix environment: people, processes, and technology.

PEOPLE

Administrators must apply security to people in terms of the roles a user performs within the organization. These user roles can include contractors, authorized users, and administrators. Other roles, such as unauthorized user or attacker, also should be considered. On the basis of these roles, different users will require different levels of logical and physical access.

Physical Security

In the context of this book, *physical security* relates to physical access to machines. Malicious users who gain physical access to a server or workstation have a much greater chance of compromising the security of that system. Administrators should restrict physical access to sensitive systems and allow access to servers only to users in roles that require access. For example, access to the servers in a Presentation Server farm should be restricted to Citrix administrators. An example of a policy to protect the physical security of servers would be to place those servers in a room that is inaccessible to everyone without an authorized access card.

For computers that cannot be placed in a restricted area, such as user workstations, an administrator must take other measures. Policies that require users to lock workstations when a user walks away and password-protected screen savers are two means of mitigating the threat of a malicious user walking up to an unattended workstation and accessing sensitive information.

Another physical security concern is the environment in which servers are stored. Servers must be protected from environmental threats such as temperature fluctuations, power surges, power outages, and fires. Administrators should use measures that regulate the environment in which servers and workstations are stored to mitigate the risk of hardware failure.

Password Policies

Part of the strength of the security of a network is a direct result of the *password policy* defined by the administrators. Password policies apply to passwords that must be chosen by and remembered by users, such as a user's primary logon credentials. Password policies also can be set for secondary applications with the use of a tool such as the Citrix Password Manager.

If an attacker can guess or otherwise obtain passwords, many other security mechanisms become entirely ineffective. The required complexity and length of a password should correspond to the privileges and data that the password protects. For example, a domain administrator account should have a stronger password than does a regular user account. A strong password policy has the following elements:

▼ Password length

■ Password complexity

■ Password history enforcement

▲ Password word usage (no dictionary words)

Another policy to consider is requiring frequent password changes. This policy is intended to prevent password guessing and cracking and to limit the amount of time during which a compromised password is useful to an attacker. If they are using a single sign-on solution such as the Password Manager, administrators can configure password changes for applications at short intervals. If users must remember their passwords, the password policy should take into account the fact that requiring changes too frequently may lead to users writing their passwords down. This can lead to password disclosure.

Least Privilege

Users in an organization have specific responsibilities associated with their roles. Administrators should grant users only the privileges that are necessary and sufficient to fulfill the obligations of their specific roles. *Least privilege* also applies to administrators. The administrator's role should be broken down into several different administrative roles, such as database administrator, mail server administrator, and network administrator. This way, if one account is compromised, the attacker does not have administrative access to the entire system.

Separation of Duties

Separation of duties is a principle stating that two roles should not have overlapping privileges and that one user should not be able to fulfill both roles. An example of this type of separation would be the requirement that a person responsible for checking for inappropriate security usage (such as an auditor) cannot make the same usages. If this happens, the user who is both administrator and auditor could violate a security policy, but no other user would be alerted to the problem.

PROCESSES

Organizations need to have processes in place for keeping their security up to date, reacting to incidents, and creating audit trails. Some processes that are specifically important in Citrix environments are security patch management, backup policies, incident response policies, and auditing policies.

Security Patch Management

Security patch management is the ongoing process of applying patches and hot fixes to the operating system and other applications. After administrators apply a patch to address a security vulnerability, a new vulnerability could occur at any time. To maintain the security of their software, administrators should implement a patch management process to ensure that their systems have all critical patches and updates installed. A typical set of steps in the patch management process (as seen in Figure 3-1) could be as follows:

▼ *Detect:* Check systems for missing security patches. This can be a manual or an automated process.

■ *Assess:* If the system requires updates, determine the severity of the threats addressed by each patch and determine if each threat requires mitigation.

■ *Acquire:* Download the patch.

■ *Test:* Deploy the patch to one server and ensure that the system works normally.

■ *Deploy:* Deploy the patch to all production servers.

▲ *Maintain:* Monitor for new patch notifications and begin the process again.

Citrix supports all Microsoft security patches. Monitor the Microsoft website for new security patches, and after a patch is released, monitor the Citrix website for information on the support of that patch.

Backup Policies

Hardware can be replaced easily, but lost user data are gone forever. Damage to a system by viruses, natural disasters, vandalism, user errors, hardware failure, and accidents cannot be predicted. In some cases, these events cannot be prevented; however, with proper *backup policies*, recovery from the events can be simplified. Administrators must have valid, complete, and up-to-date backups of their systems. The recommended method of doing this is to have a process by which the entire system is recorded onto backup media at regular intervals. The length of those intervals depends on the speed of an organization's backup equipment and the amount of storage space it has.

Administrators also should have a backup copy of their systems made on a clean installation. After an attack, administrators can use the backup to restore the system to a trusted state on a machine. Once the system has been restored to the trusted state, an administrator can close the hole through which the attacker entered the system.

Once the backups have been performed, administrators should test the backups to ensure that they are viable. They also should test to verify that they can restore backups in adverse situations. The media containing system backups must be kept in a secure location. The security measures that protect these backups should comply with the organization's security policy.

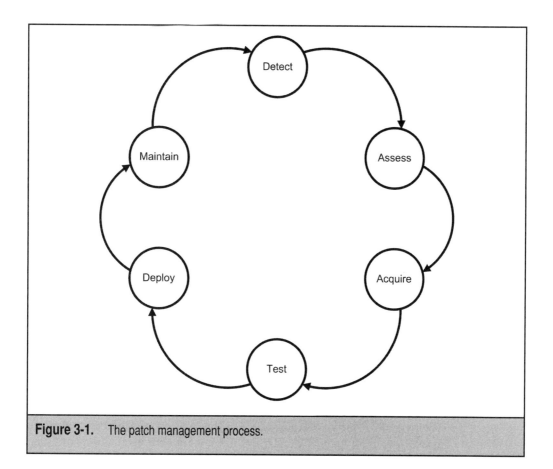

Figure 3-1. The patch management process.

Incident Response Policies

In addition to backup policies and password policies, organizations should have an *incident response policy* to deal with attacks and other incidents. This policy should include requirements for business continuity and detail ways to respond to an attack. In regard to business continuity, the incident response policy should specify whether systems can be taken offline for collection of evidence. Each system should have a priority assigned that determines what actions can be performed on that system in case of an emergency. For example, a file server could be taken offline without affecting the productivity of an organization, but a compromised mail server may have to remain online until all employees leave. A risk assessment should be performed to determine the risk of leaving each machine online versus the cost of removing it from service.

Another consideration for policy makers is under what circumstances to handle the response to an incident internally and when to contract with an outside consulting firm. If an organization chooses to handle incidents internally, it should form an incident response team. The members of that team could include a senior manager, a security officer, the network administrators, a public relations contact, and a Web administrator or other technical advisers. This team can be assembled in case of an incident and would have the capacity to respond to both the technical details and the press coverage (if applicable). The actions of the team should be governed by a specific set of rules relating to documentation, ways to secure evidence, and a list of computer forensic experts to contact in case of a crime.

After an incident is responded to, the next step in the process is recovery from that incident. Depending on the type of incident, this may include hiring new employees, restoring servers from trusted media, or instituting new policies, processes, or technologies to prevent the incident from recurring. Organizations should have predetermined recovery policies for different types of events and failures.

Auditing Policies

Log files are important to a system in that they create an audit trail, or recorded history, of the events that occur on a system or network. These trails aid auditors in tracking down problems, identifying attacks, maintaining user accountability, deterring both authorized and unauthorized users, and determining what was affected by a specific attack.

Audit trails can be reviewed either manually or by an automated process. In the case of manual review, a security policy should exist for when, why, and how these logs are viewed. Typically, the logs should be reviewed by an auditor and not by administrators because of separation of duties. A common occurrence that would require the review of audit trails would be a security incident. The incident response team would review these logs or contract with a third-party specialist to audit the logging information. Administrators also could review log files periodically to look for unusual user actions or ascertain the health of a system. Automated processes for reviewing audit trails can be used to detect either variance in normal computer usage or attack patterns in real time. Knowing that actions are logged serves as a deterrent to attackers as well as to authorized users performing unauthorized actions.

These logs are effective as a record of events and a deterrent only if their integrity is maintained. Logging should be performed on a separate server, if possible. Log files also should be secured, and access to those files should be denied to everyone but auditors. This way, no user can manipulate or delete the audit trail.

TECHNOLOGY

In addition to policies dealing with people and processes, organizations can implement technologies to enforce their security policies. Some important technologies to consider when securing a Citrix environment are antivirus software, firewalls, group policy implementations, and digital certificates.

Antivirus Software

Administrators should deploy antivirus protection on each server and desktop machine to prevent breaches in security. This protection should be present on all the machines in an organization. Thousands of new viruses and variants of those viruses are released every year, and makers of antivirus software release updates to both their virus definitions and their rule engines frequently to combat the new viruses. Antivirus software should be kept up to date by installing all new updates and patches, using the software's automatic-update feature.

Firewall Placement

Administrators have several choices relating to network layout. The choice of firewall placement is important to the overall security of the network. Firewalls can be used to restrict access between internal networks, prevent access to the internal network from

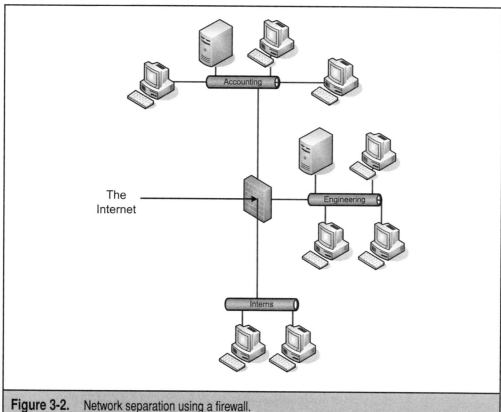

Figure 3-2. Network separation using a firewall.

the Internet, or set up a demilitarized zone (DMZ) to allow access to some servers from the Internet and disallow access to other internal network resources.

Using a firewall to restrict access between internal networks lets an administrator create different network zones for different types of users. Administrators must determine which users need access to specific resources on the basis of their roles and then deny all other access. For example, an administrator could regulate three different user roles: accountants, engineers, and interns. In some cases, interns should not have access to the Internet and engineers and finance employees may only send outgoing Internet requests. Engineers need access to the intern network but not to finance. All this configuration can be done with the use of firewalls (Figure 3-2).

DMZs can be set up in two different configurations. The first configuration option involves placing one firewall between the internal network and the Internet (Figure 3-3). This firewall would be configured to examine all incoming traffic and determine whether it should be sent to the machines in the DMZ (such as a Web server or mail server) or to the internal network.

The recommended network configuration is to deploy a dual-firewall DMZ (Figure 3-4). This configuration adds another layer of defense and isolation between the internal network and the Internet. When this architecture is used, traffic between the internal network and the Internet must traverse two firewalls. This can affect performance if there is a large amount of traffic traveling from the internal network to the Internet.

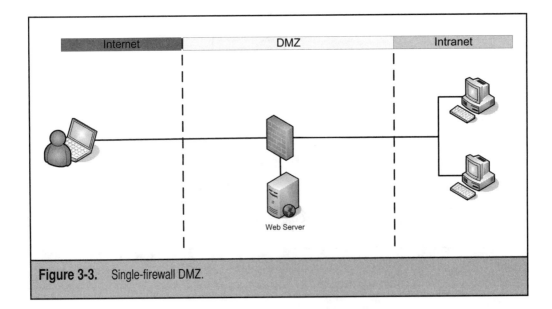

Figure 3-3. Single-firewall DMZ.

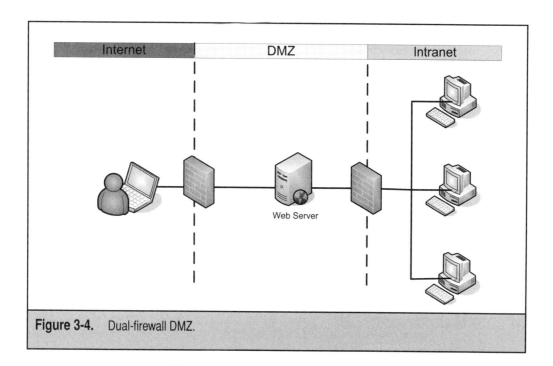

Figure 3-4.   Dual-firewall DMZ.

Secure the File System

The NTFS file system replaced the FAT32 file system on Windows NT and its derivatives: Windows 2000, Windows XP, and Windows Server 2003. This file system has several advantages over the FAT32 file system, including support for access control lists (ACLs) and the Encrypting File System. If a machine is running the FAT32 file system, an administrator can use the convert utility to convert the drive to NTFS. After this is done, administrators should set appropriate ACLs on all drive roots and operating system folders and files. All machines running Microsoft Windows that utilize Citrix software should use the NTFS file system.

Windows Group Policy

Group policy allows for centralized management of users and machines in an active directory environment. Policy-based management can be used to achieve many goals, including the following:

▼   Enable management of users and computers across the organization

■   Simplify patch management or application installations

■   Consistently implement security settings across the organization

■ Automate IT policy enforcement

▲ Implement standard desktop environments for all users

Administrators can use group policy to define configurations for different groups by creating group policy settings. This allows for one-time configuration for the administrator, after which the system can be relied on to enforce the defined policies. There are several different types of policies that can aid in remote administration.

Administrators also can use group policy to manage application installation, updates, and removal. This management can be either mandatory (assigning software to a user) or discretionary (allowing users to install software optionally by using the Add/Remove Programs Wizard). Patches and updates can be deployed through the use of group policy as well. Windows Installer can perform an install on a user's behalf. It also can restrict installations to a list of approved applications.

Administrators should review group policy and determine which of the organization's policies can be enforced through the use of group policies. Restricting users' ability to install third-party software and keeping their systems up to date is important to the overall security of the enterprise.

Certificate Management

The first selection an administrator must make when obtaining a certificate is the certificate authority (CA). Private CAs such as the Microsoft Certificate Services will issue a certificate signed by an organization's root certificate. This certificate will not be trusted by any machine outside the organization's network that has not installed the organization's root certificate but can be trusted within the network. In dealing with communication with third parties or across the Internet, administrators should use a public CA. The certificates issued by these vendors are trusted by customers and third-party software. When making this choice, administrators should determine who will be authenticated using this certificate, select which CA to trust, and be satisfied with the legal agreements that underpin that trust.

Once the CA has been selected, the administrator must choose a key length. Longer key lengths may provide greater security but increase the computation time required to encrypt or decrypt information that has been encrypted with the certificate. This may affect the time required to establish an SSL connection and the central processing unit (CPU) load on the server when establishing a connection.

Another choice an administrator must make is whether to use Server Gated Cryptography. During the period when the United States restricted the export of strong cryptography, Web browsers were shipped with this cryptography code included but disabled by default. Certain public CAs were permitted to issue certificates that used Server Gated Cryptography to unlock this cryptographic capability when communicating with specific sites. In January 2000 many of the cryptographic restrictions were removed, and newer browsers are able to use strong cryptography that is enabled by default. This makes Server Gated Cryptography applicable only to connections from older Web browsers. Administrators should always configure servers to accept connections with 128-bit encryption or greater. More expensive Server Gated Cryptography certificates no longer are required.

SUMMARY

To secure their enterprise systems, administrators should implement common best practices. The information in this book provides the basis for understanding this issue. Armed with this knowledge, administrators can make informed decisions about what assets must be protected on their systems and the multiple ways those assets can be protected.

CHAPTER 4

Secure Gateway

T his chapter explains how to protect the Secure Gateway for Windows. The discussion covers the assets of the Secure Gateway, threats to those assets, countermeasures to the threats, and instructions for implementing the counter-measures in a Citrix environment.

DEPLOYMENTS

Figure 4-1 shows a Secure Gateway deployment that is used to provide secure access from a client device to a Citrix Presentation Server farm. The client device runs a Web browser and a Presentation Server Client and resides on the Internet. The Secure Gateway and the Web Interface reside on the DMZ. The server farm, with at least one Presentation Server running the Secure Ticket Authority (STA), resides on the intranet. Firewalls separate the Internet from the DMZ and the DMZ from the intranet.

Figure 4-2 shows a Secure Gateway deployment that is used to provide secure access from a client device to a Presentation Server farm, with the Secure Gateway in front of the Web Interface. The client device runs a Web browser and the Presentation Server Client and resides on the Internet. Both the Secure Gateway and the Web Interface reside on the DMZ. The server farm, with at least one Presentation Server running the STA, resides on the intranet. Firewalls separate the Internet from the DMZ and the DMZ from the intranet. The difference between this deployment and the one shown in Figure 4-1 is that the Web Interface is behind the Secure Gateway. This offers the benefit of not expos-ing the Web Interface directly to Internet traffic, but limits the functionality of the Web Interface. See Chapter 2, "Secure Deployments," and Chapter 5, "Web Interface," for more information.

COMPONENTS

Secure Gateway

The Secure Gateway is a software component that is included with the Citrix Presenta-tion Server which provides a mechanism for remote users to access published appli-cations securely through a DMZ. The Secure Gateway resides in the DMZ, relays au-thenticated ICA connections, and prevents unauthenticated ICA traffic from reaching an organization's intranet. Using the Secure Gateway allows administrators to ensure that only authenticated users access applications and data from an organization's server farm.

NOTE   Citrix Access Gateway is a separate product and is delivered as an appliance. For more information on Citrix Access Gateway, see Appendix A, "Other Citrix Solutions."

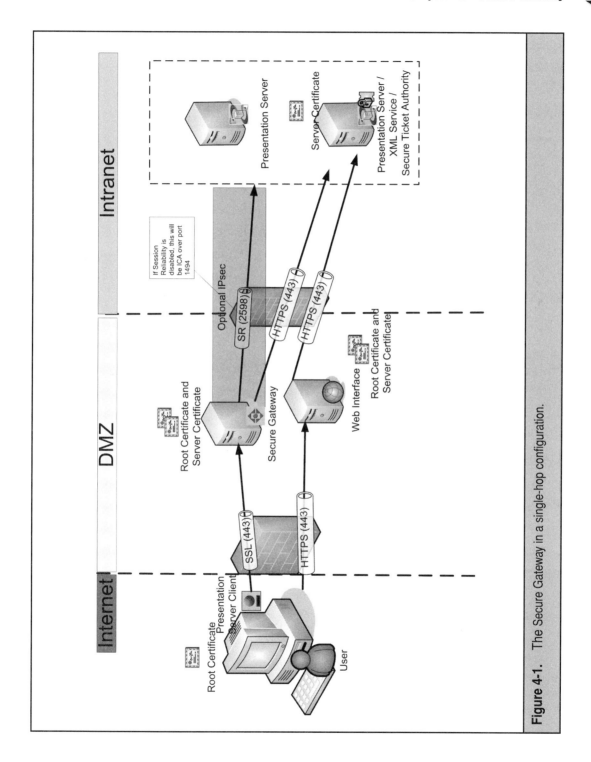

Figure 4-1. The Secure Gateway in a single-hop configuration.

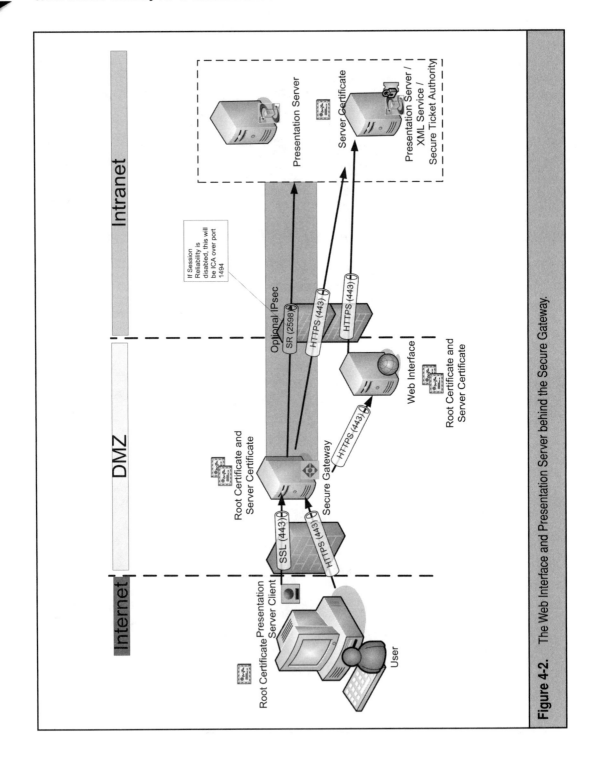

Figure 4-2. The Web Interface and Presentation Server behind the Secure Gateway.

Secure Gateway Proxy

For organizations that utilize two DMZs, the Secure Gateway Proxy provides a relay between the Secure Gateway, which is installed in the first DMZ, and the server farm on the intranet. The Secure Gateway Proxy acts as a conduit for traffic from the Secure Gateway to servers on the intranet, allowing only authenticated ICA traffic to travel from the Internet to the server farm.

Figure 4-3 shows a Secure Gateway deployment that is used to provide secure access from a client device to a Presentation Server farm, with the Secure Gateway in a double-hop DMZ deployment. The Secure Gateway resides in the first DMZ. The Secure Gateway Proxy and the Web Interface reside in the second DMZ. The server farm, with at least one Presentation Server running the STA, resides on the intranet. Firewalls separate the Internet from the first DMZ, the first DMZ from the second DMZ, and the second DMZ from the intranet. This offers the benefit of not exposing the Web Interface directly to Internet traffic but limits the functionality of the Web Interface. The Secure Gateway Proxy functions as a relay in this deployment, allowing traffic from the Secure Gateway to the intranet. See Chapter 2, "Secure Deployments," and Chapter 5, "Web Interface," for more information.

SECURE GATEWAY ASSETS

The Secure Gateway has the following assets:

▼ *Access to the intranet.* The security characteristics of this asset are confidentiality and availability.

■ *Session data between clients and the Secure Gateway.* The security characteristics of this asset are confidentiality and integrity.

■ *Configuration of the Secure Gateway.* The security characteristics of this asset are confidentiality and integrity.

■ *Session data between clients and the Presentation Server.* The security characteristics of this asset are confidentiality, integrity, and availability.

■ *Log files.* The security characteristics of this asset are confidentiality and integrity.

■ *Server certificate (used to protect traffic from the client to the Secure Gateway).* The security characteristic of this asset is integrity. The corresponding security characteristic of the private key is confidentiality.

■ *Secure Gateway Service.* The security characteristics of this asset are availability and integrity.

■ *Session data between the Secure Gateway and the Presentation Server.* The security characteristics of this asset are confidentiality and integrity.

■ *Session data between the Secure Gateway and the Secure Gateway Proxy (if applicable).* The security characteristics of this asset are confidentiality and integrity.

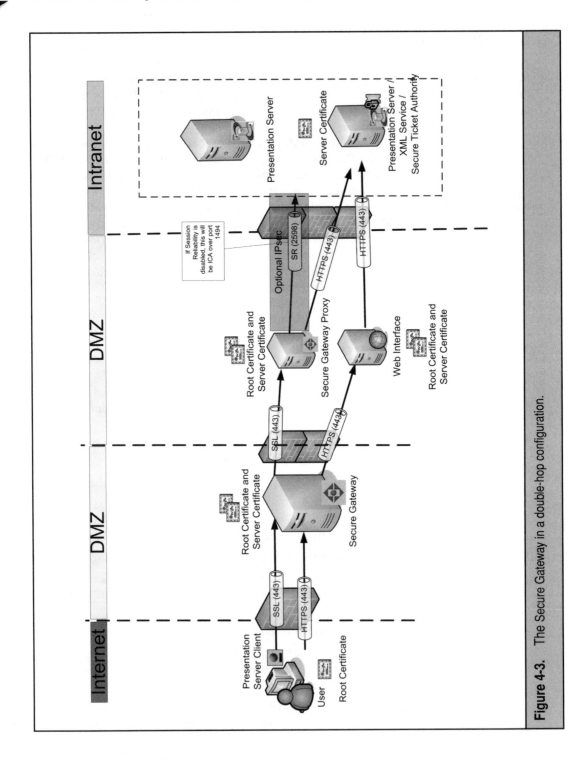

Figure 4-3. The Secure Gateway in a double-hop configuration.

- *Session data between the Secure Gateway and the Web Interface.* The security characteristics of this asset are confidentiality and integrity.

- *The Web Interface session data.* The security characteristics of this asset are confidentiality and integrity.

▲ *Session data between the Secure Gateway or Secure Gateway Proxy and the Secure Ticket Authority*. The security characteristics of this asset are confidentiality and integrity.

THREATS AND COUNTERMEASURES

As an Internet-facing component, the Secure Gateway is a target for external attackers. If an attacker penetrates the Secure Gateway, that attacker is significantly closer to penetrating the intranet. The following are the main threats against the Secure Gateway:

▼ Service disruption

■ Unauthorized access to the Secure Gateway

■ Compromise of session data between the client and the gateway

■ Compromise of session data between the Secure Gateway and the Presentation Server

■ Compromise of session data between the Secure Gateway and the Secure Gateway Proxy

■ Compromise of session data between the Secure Gateway or Secure Gateway Proxy and the Secure Ticket Authority

■ Compromise of session data between the Secure Gateway and the Web Interface

■ Compromise of session data between a client Web browser and the Web Interface

■ Tampering with the Secure Gateway configuration

■ Unauthorized access to log files

▲ Worms, viruses, and other malicious software

Service Disruption

Service disruptions must be planned for. They can be caused by nonmalicious or malicious activity. Service disruptions can be caused by the following:

▼ System failure

■ Software failure

■ Hardware failures

■ Power failure

■ Human error

■ Accidental deletion of files

■ Misconfiguration

▲ Malicious behavior

■ Denial-of-service attacks

Countermeasures

Countermeasures to nonmalicious disruptions in service include the following:

▼ Restricting access to Secure Gateway administration functions

▲ Backups

Countermeasures to denial of service attacks include audit trails.

Restricting access to Secure Gateway administrative functionality limits the damage that any single person can do. Backups allow for recovery from disruption of service and malicious software. Proper audit trails provide a mechanism for recognizing an attack and identifying any authenticated users who may be involved.

Unauthorized Access to the Secure Gateway

Unauthorized access to the Secure Gateway occurs when a user executes Secure Gateway administrative functionality in violation of the organization's policies. Attackers can gain unauthorized access to Secure Gateway services in several ways:

▼ Physically access the Secure Gateway.

■ Remotely attack the Secure Gateway.

▲ Remotely log in to the Secure Gateway.

If an attacker physically accesses the Secure Gateway, several attacks are possible, such as the following:

▼ Restart the machine and use various tools to circumvent operating system security.

▲ Log in at the console.

If someone can remotely send traffic to the Secure Gateway, that person can launch network-based attacks against the operating system and services running on the server.

The goal of these remote attacks may be to log in remotely to the Secure Gateway host. If someone can log in remotely to the Secure Gateway host, that person can

▼ View the event logs.

▲ Tamper with the configuration of the Secure Gateway.

Countermeasures

Countermeasures to unauthorized access to Secure Gateway include the following:

▼ Restrict who can physically reach the Secure Gateway.

■ Restrict the number of Windows accounts on the Secure Gateway host.

▲ Set appropriate ACLs on configuration and log files.

To prevent unauthorized access to the Secure Gateway, provide access to the Secure Gateway host only to those who need it. The goal is to limit the access those users have and prevent them from logging in to or executing unauthorized administrative functions on the Secure Gateway. These countermeasures help limit the number of users who can do damage and minimize the damage a user can do.

Compromise of Client to Gateway Session Data

Any time information is sent over a public network such as the Internet, there is a risk that it can be intercepted. There are several threats to such traffic:

▼ Information disclosure

■ Tampering

▲ Disruption

An attacker may seek to prevent a client's traffic from traversing the Internet. Countermeasures to this type of attack are beyond the scope of this book.

Countermeasures

Countermeasures to these threats include using the Secure Gateway. The Secure Gateway provides a countermeasure to information disclosure and tampering by using SSL/TLS for all client-to-gateway communication. By design, SSL/TLS prevents information disclosure (other than that traffic is being sent) and tampering.

Compromise of Secure Gateway to Presentation Server Session Data

As with traffic sent across the Internet, traffic on local networks can be intercepted. The threats are the same:

▼ Information disclosure

■ Tampering

▲ Disruption

Countermeasures

Countermeasures to these threats include the following:

▼ Use IPsec between the Secure Gateway and Presentation Servers.

▲ Protect the network from disruption.

To prevent information disclosure or tampering, administrators may use IPsec, which is a standard feature of Windows, between the Secure Gateway and the Presentation Server. IPsec can authenticate the hosts involved and prevent unauthorized hosts from masquerading as authorized hosts. Using IPsec allows administrators to ensure that session data that is passing through the Secure Gateway is sent only to legitimate Presentation Servers. Administrators can protect their networks from disruption by employing standard network best practices.

Compromise of Session Data Between Secure Gateway and Secure Gateway Proxy

Sending information over a network exposes the data to various threats. Those threats include:

▼ Information disclosure

■ Tampering

▲ Disruption

Countermeasures

Countermeasures to these threats include the following:

▼ Protect the network from disruption.

▲ Use SSL/TLS between the Secure Gateway and the Secure Gateway Proxy.

Administrators using the Secure Gateway can mitigate or eliminate each of these threats by employing standard networking best practices. The Secure Gateway provides a countermeasure to information disclosure or tampering by using SSL/TLS for all communication between the Secure Gateway and the Secure Gateway Proxy. This creates a secure connection from the Secure Gateway to the Secure Gateway Proxy.

Compromise of Session Data Between Secure Gateway/Secure Gateway Proxy and Secure Ticket Authority

The Secure Gateway and the Secure Gateway Proxy use the Secure Ticket Authority to authenticate connections from clients. Attackers may seek to compromise this traffic to:

▼ Deny an authorized user access

▲ Allow an unauthorized user access

Countermeasures

Countermeasures to these threats include the following:

▼ Protect the network from disruption.

▲   Use SSL/TLS between the Secure Gateway or Secure Gateway Proxy and the STA.

Administrators can protect their networks against disruption by using standard networking best practices. To protect traffic between the Secure Gateway or Secure Gateway Proxy and the Secure Ticket Authority from tampering, administrators should enable SSL/TLS in the Secure Gateway Configuration Wizard. This creates a secure communication channel between the Secure Gateway or Secure Gateway Proxy and the Secure Ticket Authority.

Compromise of Session Data Between Secure Gateway and the Web Interface

Sending information over a network exposes the data to various threats. Those threats include:

▼   Disruption

■   Information disclosure

▲   Tampering

Countermeasures

Countermeasures to these threats include the following:

▼   Protect the network from disruption.

▲   Use SSL/TLS between the Secure Gateway and the Web Interface.

Administrators can protect their networks from disruption by employing standard network best practices. The Secure Gateway provides a countermeasure to information disclosure or tampering by using SSL/TLS for all communication from the Secure Gateway to the Web Interface. This creates a secure connection from the Secure Gateway to the Web Interface.

Compromise of Session Data Between Client Web Browser and Web Interface

Administrators who are concerned about the security of traffic from remote Web browsers to the Web Interface should consult Chapter 5, "Web Interface." It discusses this issue in more detail and provides recommendations for administrators who want to secure their Web Interface deployments.

Tampering with Secure Gateway Configuration

The Secure Gateway's configuration data, which are stored in files in C:\Program Files\ Citrix\Secure Gateway\conf\, may be targeted by attackers who hope to modify the behavior of the Secure Gateway. The settings configured in the Secure Gateway Configuration Wizard are stored in the configuration file. An attacker who modifies the configuration file can tamper with settings such as whether SSL/TLS should be enabled.

Countermeasures

Countermeasures against tampering of configuration files include the following:

▼   Restrict access to the configuration files.

▲   Use audit trails.

Restricting access may be done by limiting which users can log in to the Secure Gateway machine and by using audit trails.

Administrators should have the following permissions to the configuration files:

▼   Modify

■   Read & Execute

■   List Folder Contents

■   Read

▲   Write

The account selected by the administrator, preferably Network Service, for Secure Gateway to run as needs:

▼   Read & Execute

■   List Folder Contents

▲   Read

Setting these ACLs limits the number of people who can modify the configuration file. It also limits the amount of damage any single individual can do.

Unauthorized Access to Log Files

The Secure Gateway log files, which are located in C:\Program Files\Citrix\Secure Gateway\logs, are valuable when an incident occurs. The Secure Gateway log files face the following threats:

▼   Disclosure

■   Tampering

▲   Destruction

Disclosure of log files may reveal information about an organization such as the following:

▼   User names

- Client IP addresses
- Client session start time
- Client session end time
- Client session status
- Presentation Server IP addresses
- Port numbers used by Presentation Servers
- ▲ Protocol used by client

Tampering with log files allows an attacker to conceal his or her activity. Destruction of log files is a threat because it eliminates the audit trail completely.

Countermeasures

Countermeasures to prevent unauthorized access to log files include the following:

- ▼ Limit the number of users who have access to the Secure Gateway machine.
- ▲ Set ACLs on the log files.

Limiting access to the log files helps prevent disclosure and tampering. The user account that Secure Gateway runs as needs **Write** permissions to the logs directory. Only administrative users should have access to this machine.

Secure Gateway also uses the Windows Event Log service to record events, which only administrators have access. The Windows Event logs also have the property of being append-only, which inhibits tampering by allowing information only to be added, not modified. To protect logs further from tampering or destruction, they should be backed up to another machine or to removable media.

Worms, Viruses, and Other Malicious Software

Malicious software on the Secure Gateway can disrupt the availability of the services of the Secure Gateway and pose a threat to other machines in the DMZ and the intranet.

Countermeasures

Countermeasures against malicious software include

- ▼ Protective network-based hardware
- Protective network-based software
- Protective host-based software
- ▲ Limiting the exposure of the Secure Gateway

Protective network-based hardware such as a firewall helps prevent unauthorized communication with the Secure Gateway. Some protective network-based software, such as intrusion prevention systems, attempts to prevent attack traffic from reaching hosts. Intrusion detection systems monitor for suspicious activity and can be network-based, host-based, or both. Similarly, host-based software such as antivirus software and antispyware software helps prevent malicious software from damaging the server. To limit the exposure of the Secure Gateway, do not run software such as Web browsers or instant messaging clients from the Secure Gateway.

STEPS FOR SECURING SECURE GATEWAY

The following steps for securing the Secure Gateway are discussed below:

▼ Secure the operating system.

■ Configure the Secure Gateway Configuration Wizard

■ Install the Secure Gateway as a nonprivileged user.

■ Restrict access to the Secure Gateway.

■ Enable IPsec between the Secure Gateway and the Presentation Server.

■ Protect the log files.

▲ Configure auditing.

Secure the Operating System

The Windows 2003 Security Configuration Wizard allows administrators to secure the operating system. It provides a mechanism to lock down ports used by various services and disable Windows services that are unnecessary. The options that appear while one is running the Windows Server 2003 Security Configuration Wizard vary with the choices made in each step.

NOTE Administrators may have to modify these steps to account for installed software such as antivirus or firewall software.

To install and run the Security Configuration Wizard, do the following:

1. Log on to the server as a Windows administrator.

2. Launch the Add or Remove Programs tool (**Start > Control Panel > Add or Remove Programs**).

3. Click **Add/Remove Windows Components** to bring up the **Windows Components Wizard**.

4. Select the **Security Configuration Wizard** check box and click **Next**. A number of progress messages temporarily appear.

5. When the installation is complete, click **Finish**.

6. Close the **Add or Remove Programs** dialog box.

7. Launch the Security Configuration Wizard **(Start > Administrative Tools > Security Configuration Wizard)**.

8. At the **Welcome** screen, click **Next**.

9. At the **Configuration Action** screen, ensure that **Create a New Security Policy** is selected and click **Next**.

10. At the **Select Server** screen, leave the default value and click **Next**.

11. At the **Processing Security Configuration Database** screen, wait for the system scan to complete and click **Next**.

12. At the **Role-Based Service Configuration** screen, click **Next**.

13. The options administrators should select from the **Select Server Roles** screen vary with the machine to which they are applying the Security Configuration Wizard. Each of the subsequent screens requires the selection of different options, as shown in Table 4-1.

Screen	Options
Select Server Roles	Clear all roles and click **Next**.
Select Client Features	DNS Client
Select Administration and Other Options	Windows firewall
Select Additional Services	Secure Gateway
Handling Unspecified Services	Do not change the start-up mode of the service.
Confirm Service Changes	Click **Next**.
Network Security	Leave **Skip this section** cleared and click **Next**.
	Open Ports and Approved Applications 443(HTTPS)
	Ports used by Secure Gateway (CtxSGSvc.exe)
Confirm Port Configuration	Click **Next**.
Registry Settings	Leave **Skip this section** cleared and click **Next**.
Require SMB Security Signatures	Leave **All computers that connect to it satisfy the minimum operating system requirements** checked.

(continued on next page)

Table 4-1.   Security Configuration Wizard

Screen	Options
	Leave **It has surplus process capacity that can be used to sign the file and print traffic** checked.
	Click **Next**.
Outbound Authentication Methods	Clear all methods and click **Next**.
Inbound Authentication Methods	Clear both check boxes and click **Next**.
Registry Settings Summary	Click **Next**.
Audit Policy	Leave the **Skip this section** check box cleared and click **Next**.
	Select **Audit successful and unsuccessful activities**.
	Click **Next**.

Table 4-1.   Security Configuration Wizard (continued)

Install Secure Gateway as a Nonprivileged User

When installing the Secure Gateway, administrators can select the user account that the Secure Gateway Service will run as. Administrators should select a nonprivileged account such as Network Service. This helps limit the damage that can be done by someone who compromises the Secure Gateway Service.

Configure the Secure Gateway Configuration Wizard

The Secure Gateway Configuration Wizard allows administrators to modify settings for the Secure Gateway. Many of these settings are security-related.

To run the Secure Gateway Configuration Wizard, do the following:

1. Be sure a server certificate is installed on the Secure Gateway.

2. Start the Secure Gateway Configuration Wizard (**Start** > **All Programs** > **Citrix** > **Administration Tools** > **Secure Gateway Configuration Wizard**).

3. The options administrators should make selections in the wizard in accordance with the organization's security policy. Each of the subsequent screens requires selection of different options according to Table 4-2.

Screen	Options
Welcome to the Secure Gateway Configuration Wizard	Administrators should select which products they want to secure and then click **OK**.
Secure Gateway configuration level	Choose **Advanced** to configure the options below. Administrators using a deployment that requires users to connect directly to the Web Interface should check **Enable direct access to the Web Interface**. Click **Next**.
Select a server certificate	Administrators should select a server certificate from the list. If none appears, administrators need to obtain and install a server certificate before proceeding. Click **Next**.
Configure secure protocol settings	**Transport Layer Security (TLSv1)**. To allow clients to use either SSLv3 or TLSv1, choose **Secure Sockets Layer (SSLv3 and TLSv1)**. To require that clients use only FIPS-140-compliant encryption algorithms (RSA_WITH_3DES_EDE_CBC_SHA), choose **GOV**. To use the commercial cipher suite (RSA_WITH_RC4_128_MD5 or RSA_WITH_RC4_128_SHA), select **COM**. To allow the client to use either cipher suite, select **ALL**. Click **Next**.
Configure inbound client connections	Select either Monitor all IP addresses or the appropriate external interface(s) and click **Next**.
Configure server(s) running the Secure Gateway Proxy (double-hop configuration only)	Click **Add** and enter the Fully Qualified Domain Name (FQDN) or IP address of a machine running the Secure Gateway Proxy. Repeat this for all machines running the Secure Gateway Proxy. Check **Secure traffic between the Secure Gateway and Secure Gateway Proxy**. Click **OK**.

(continued on next page)

Table 4-2.   Secure Gateway Configuration Wizard

Screen	Options
Configure outbound connections (for ACL only)	Click **Add** and enter the IP range and protocol for each outbound connection that should be allowed. Click **Next**.
Authentication Service Details	Enter the FQDN of the Authentication Service. Check **Secure traffic between Secure Gateway and the Authentication Service**. Click **Next**.
Connection parameters	Click **Next**.
Logging exclusions	Click **Next**.
Details of the server running the Logon Agent	Check **Secure traffic between Secure Gateway and the Logon Agent**.
Logging parameters	Select one of the following: *Fatal events only:* Logs only events that stop the Secure Gateway from functioning. Use this only if log space is very limited. *Error and fatal events:* Logs only errors and fatal events. Use this to record only definite problems. *Warning, error, and fatal events:* For warnings and errors. Use this to log most events. *All events, including informational:* Logs all warnings, errors, fatal events, and Secure Gateway traces. Use this for complete logs, but be aware that this can produce large logs.
Secure Gateway configuration complete	Click **Finish**.

Table 4-2.   Secure Gateway Configuration Wizard (continued)

Restrict Access to Secure Gateway

To protect the Secure Gateway configuration, it is important to limit which users have access to administrative functions. There are two places where a person can access administrative functions: over the network and locally at the machine.

Limit Network Access to Secure Gateway

As was shown in the figures earlier in this chapter, anyone on the Internet can send Secure Gateway traffic. The Secure Gateway communicates with clients by using SSL/

TLS on port 443. To match the secure deployment, a firewall must be placed between the Internet and the Secure Gateway to block all other traffic. Similarly, administrators should place a firewall behind the Secure Gateway to limit the possibility of an attack from within the intranet. This also limits the damage that can be done by an attacker who compromises the Secure Gateway machine.

Assign Secure Gateway to Its Own Workgroup

The Secure Gateway should be installed as a workgroup machine. It does not need to be a member of a domain. Administrators who need access to the machine should have local accounts.

Enable IPsec Between Secure Gateway and Presentation Server

To protect traffic between the Secure Gateway and the Presentation Server, administrators can use IPsec. This prevents an attacker from reading traffic between the Secure Gateway and the Presentation Server and detects any tampering with the traffic. Using IPsec also prevents an attacker from impersonating a valid Presentation Server or Secure Gateway to intercept traffic. For more information on setting up IPsec, administrators should view the Microsoft documentation available at http://www.microsoft.com.

Protect Log Files

To help prevent attackers from reading or tampering with log files, administrators should protect log files with proper ACLs and backups. The Secure Gateway uses the Windows Security Event log to record events, which by default on Windows 2003 is accessible only by administrators. Windows Event logs are append-only to prevent modification. However, administrators or attackers who have gained administrative privileges can clear the logs. The Secure Gateway also creates log files in C:\Program Files\Citrix\Secure Gateway\logs. Administrators should ensure that

▼ The user account Secure Gateway that is running has **Write** permissions to the logs directory.

▲ Only administrators have **Read** and **List Folder Contents** permissions to the logs directory.

To protect log data from loss, the logs should be backed up regularly.

Configure Auditing

Internet-facing applications such as the Secure Gateway must be monitored carefully. Administrators should monitor the following events:

▼ Administrator logon

■ Unsuccessful logon attempts by administrators or remote clients

▲ Invalid ticket warnings

The Windows Security Event log should be used to track administrator logons. Administrators should log on only from the local console.

Failed attempts to log on by administrators will be logged by Windows in the Windows Security Event log. If a remote client attempts to log on and fails, the Secure Gateway will log that in the access log. Failed logon attempts are especially important, as they may indicate attempts to break into the Secure Gateway, and they should be dealt with accordingly.

The Secure Gateway checks the validity of the tickets used by clients to authenticate their traffic. If the Secure Gateway encounters an invalid ticket, a **Warning** message will be generated in the access log.

VERIFY SECURED CONFIGURATION

To verify that all the security steps have been followed, do the following:

1. From a machine within each DMZ, run a port scanner and verify that only the expected ports are open on the Secure Gateway.

2. From a machine within each DMZ, run a port scanner and verify that only the expected ports are open on the Secure Gateway Proxy.

3. From a machine on the Internet, run a port scanner and verify that only the expected ports are open.

4. From a machine within the intranet, run a port scanner and verify that only the expected ports are open on the Secure Gateway.

5. Make sure that regular backups are being made.

6. Using a third-party network monitor, start a network capture and record as users connect to the Secure Gateway from outside the intranet. Confirm that the traffic is encrypted with SSL/TLS and that it is using the appropriate cipher suite (for example, a FIPS 140-compliant cipher suite).

7. If the Secure Gateway Proxy is installed, use a network monitor, start a network capture, and record traffic between the Secure Gateway and the Secure Gateway Proxy. Confirm that the traffic is encrypted by using SSL/TLS and that it is using the appropriate cipher suite (for example, a FIPS 140-compliant cipher suite).

8. Using a network monitor, start a network capture and record traffic between the Secure Gateway and the Web Interface. Confirm that the traffic is encrypted with SSL/TLS and that it is using the appropriate cipher suite (for example, a FIPS 140-compliant cipher suite).

9. Using a third-party network monitor, start a network capture and record traffic between the Secure Gateway or Secure Gateway Proxy and the Presentation Server. Confirm that the traffic is encrypted using IPsec.

SUMMARY

This chapter explored threats to the Secure Gateway and countermeasures to each of those threats and has shown how to implement each countermeasure. Always keep the operating system, antivirus software, and the Secure Gateway up to date with the latest security hot fixes and service packs.

CHAPTER 5

Web Interface

This chapter explains how to protect the Web Interface server. The discussion covers the assets of the Web Interface, threats to those assets, countermeasures to the threats, and instructions for implementing the countermeasures in a Presentation Server environment.

The Web Interface provides users with access to applications hosted on the Presentation Server through a standard Web browser or through the Program Neighborhood Agent.

The Web Interface dynamically creates a Hyper Text Markup Language (HTML) depiction of server farms for Presentation Server sites. Users are presented with all the applications published in the server farm or farms that are accessible to them.

Additionally, the Web Interface allows an administrator to configure settings for users who are accessing applications through the Program Neighborhood Agent.

The Web Interface can be configured by using the Access Suite Console or by directly editing the configuration file (WebInterface.conf). This allows the creation and management of Presentation Server farms, the configuration of client access and control, authentication methods such as two-factor authentication mechanisms, and control over ICA session configuration.

DEPLOYMENTS

When used with a Citrix Presentation Server Client, the Web Interface provides a single point of access to published applications. Refer to Chapter 8, "Presentation Server Client," for further information. The Web Interface also can provide settings and application information to the Program Neighborhood Agent, which will populate a user's program menu with published applications.

In the basic deployment of the Web Interface, a user, employing a standard Web browser or the Program Neighborhood Agent, communicates with the Web Interface server by using HTTP. When the user logs on to the Web Interface, the Web Interface server passes the credentials to the Presentation Server for authentication via the eXtensible Markup Language (XML) service. Once the user is authenticated, the Presentation Server returns the list of applications for that user to the Web Interface, and the Web Interface server displays the list of applications to the user. Once the user clicks on an application, the Web Interface server builds an ICA file and passes it back to the client. The Presentation Server Client interprets the ICA file, allowing it to launch the application by contacting the Presentation Server directly on port 1494 or on port 2598 if Session Reliability is enabled. Refer to Chapter 7, "Presentation Server," for more information on session reliability. The following figures explain different deployment scenarios.

Figure 5-1 shows a secured deployment of a Web Interface. The client connects to the Web Interface server by using HTTPS, and all communications between the Web Interface server and the Presentation Server are secured with SSL/TLS, using the process shown here.

Another variation of this deployment is to use the Secure Gateway (Figure 5-2). This allows a single point of entry for Web Interface connections and Presentation Server connections.

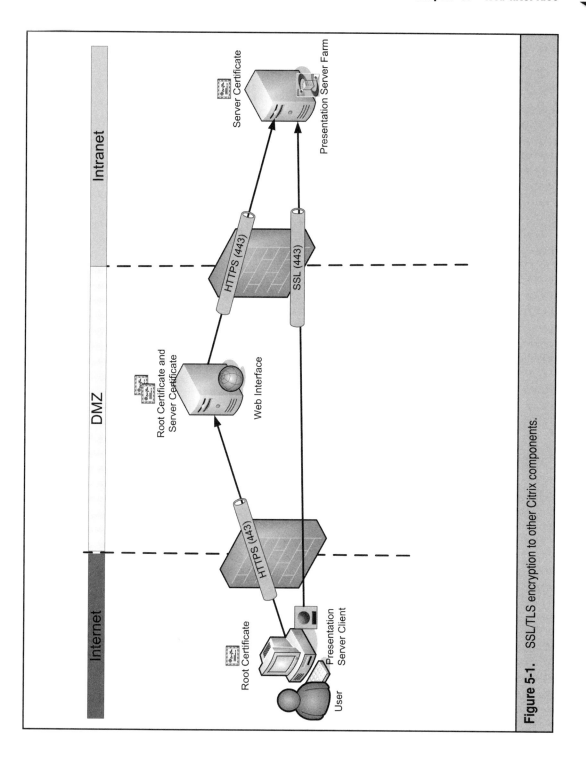

Figure 5-1. SSL/TLS encryption to other Citrix components.

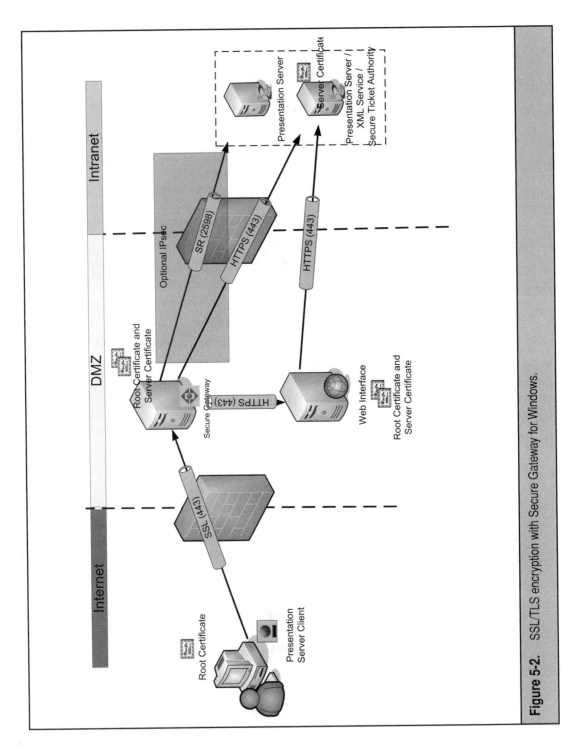

Figure 5-2. SSL/TLS encryption with Secure Gateway for Windows.

Figure 5-3 shows a deployment of the Web Interface server in an IPsec environment. All communications between the Web Interface, the Secure Gateway, and the Presentation Server are encrypted by using IPsec. The client connects to the Web Interface via the Secure Gateway, using SSL or TLS.

Figure 5-4 shows that only the communication between the client's browser and the Web Interface is secured by using HTTPS. After the user launches an application, the client connects directly to the server that is running the Presentation Server, using Transmission Control Protocol (TCP) port 1494 or port 2598 if session reliability is used.

COMPONENTS

The Web Interface provides users with access to Presentation Server applications and content through a standard Web browser or through the Program Neighborhood Agent. The system consists of several components that work in concert.

Web Interface

The Web Interface is a component that provides a point of access to one or more Presentation Server farms. The configuration file can be edited locally using a text editor. The configuration file can also be stored on a centralized data store, allowing control of several Web Interface servers from a single Access Suite Console and allowing easier backup of the configuration file for those Web Interface servers.

Web Interface Configuration File

The Web Interface configuration file contains all configuration information for the Web Interface server. The configuration file can be edited locally or remotely by using the Access Suite Console. The configuration file also can be stored on a centralized data store, allowing control of several Web Interface servers from a single Access Suite Console and allowing easier backup of the configuration file for those Web Interface servers.

Access Suite Console

The Access Suite Console is a Microsoft Management Console (MMC) snap-in for the Web Interface. This snap-in provides remote administration of the Web Interface.

ICA File

The ICA file is generated on the Web Interface server from a template ICA file when a user launches an application. The Presentation Server or Secure Gateway address is added along with session configuration parameters. These parameters control various aspects of the client session, such as window size. The ICA file then is downloaded to the client.

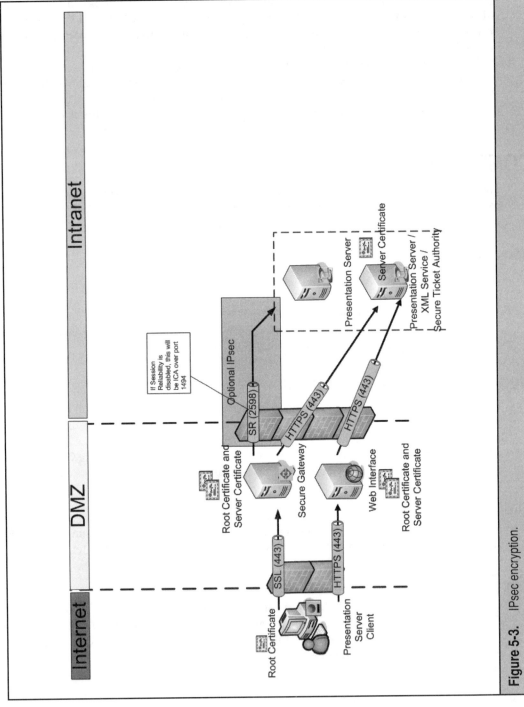

Figure 5-3. IPsec encryption.

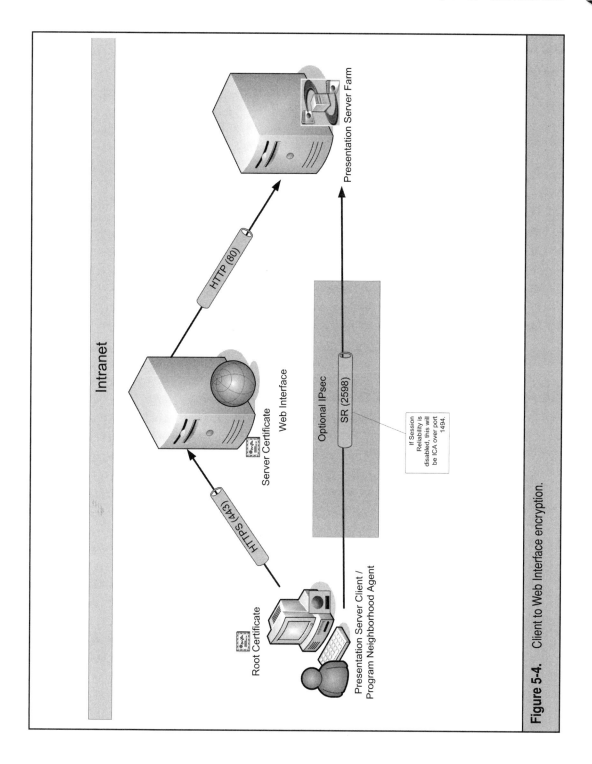

Figure 5-4.   Client to Web Interface encryption.

ASSETS

The Web Interface has the following assets:

▼ *Web Interface service.* The security characteristics of this asset are availability, integrity, and auditability.

■ *Configuration file.* The security characteristics of this asset are confidentiality, integrity, and auditability.

■ *Session data.* The security characteristics of this asset are confidentiality and integrity.

■ *ICA files.* The security characteristics of this asset are confidentiality and integrity.

■ *Log files.* The security characteristics of these files are confidentiality and integrity.

■ *User credentials* (passwords, PINs, certificates). The security characteristic of these assets is confidentiality.

■ *XML service communication.* The security characteristics of this asset are confidentiality and integrity.

▲ *Secure Gateway communication.* The security characteristics of this asset are confidentiality and integrity.

THREATS AND COUNTERMEASURES

As an Internet-facing component, the Web Interface is a target for external attackers. If an attacker penetrates the Web Interface, the attacker will be significantly closer to penetrating the intranet. The following are the main threats against the Web Interface:

▼ Unauthorized access to the Web Interface

■ Service disruption

■ Disclosure of the ICA file

■ Tampering with configuration files

■ Profiling

▲ Worms, viruses, and other malicious software

Unauthorized Access to Web Interface

Unauthorized access occurs when a user executes restricted Web Interface functions that organizational policies do not explicitly authorize that user to execute. Attackers can gain unauthorized access in two ways:

▼ Gaining physical access to the machine

▲ Remotely connecting to the server

If an attacker physically accesses the Web Interface server, that person can perform a variety of malicious tasks, such as the following:

▼   Restarting the machine and using various tools to circumvent operating system security

▲   Logging into the console

If someone has remote access to the server, that person can

▼   Attempt to modify the Web Interface configuration

■   Launch network-based attacks against the operating system and services running on the server

■   Launch a denial-of-service attack against the server

■   View the log files

▲   Deface the Web Interface pages

Countermeasures

Preventing unauthorized access to the Web Interface server means that only those who need access to the Web Interface server can get it. Separation of roles is important. Individuals who are responsible for maintaining the hardware of the Web Interface server may not need to configure users on the Web Interface server. Windows administrators may need physical access to the machine, but this can be supervised by those responsible for hardware maintenance. Web Interface server administrators do not need to be Windows administrators and do not require physical access to the machine.

Countermeasures to unauthorized access to the Web Interface server service include the following:

▼   Limit who can reach (physically and remotely) the Web Interface server.

■   Set an appropriate ACL on configuration and log files.

▲   Use SSL/TLS for administrative network communication to and from the server.

These countermeasures help limit the number of users who can do damage and the amount of damage a single user can do.

Service Disruption

Service disruptions must be planned for. They can be caused by nonmalicious or malicious activity. Service disruptions can have several causes:

▼   *System failure*

    ■ Software failures

    ■ Hardware failures

- Power failures
- *Human error*
  - Accidental deletion of files
  - Misconfiguration
- *Malicious behavior*
  - Denial-of-service attacks

Countermeasures

Countermeasures to nonmalicious service disruptions include the following:

▼ Restrict access to Web Interface administration functions.

▲ Use backups.

Countermeasures to denial-of-service attacks include audit trails.

Restricting access to Web Interface administrative functionality limits the damage that any single person can do. Backups allow for recovery from service disruptions and malicious software. Proper audit trails provide a mechanism for recognizing an attack and identifying any authenticated users who may be involved.

Disclosure of ICA File

The disclosure of an ICA file may reveal Presentation Server network addresses, login tickets, and published application names. This could assist an attacker's attempt to gain unauthorized access to the Presentation Server farm. ICA file contents can be disclosed in several ways:

▼ Interception on the network

▲ Saving ICA files to an unsecured client machine

Countermeasures

Several methods can be used to prevent ICA file disclosure or to protect important details within the ICA file:

▼ Enable SSL/TLS.

■ Enable STA tickets.

▲ Enable the automatic deletion of ICA files.

Encrypting the network traffic between the client and the Web Interface server will prevent the ICA file from being intercepted. The STA replaces server addresses with session tickets. This has two advantages: The Presentation Server address is hidden from the client, and the session ticket has an expiration time after which the ICA file is useless. Refer to Chapter 7, "Presentation Server," for further information about the STA.

The Web Interface server also sets a flag in the ICA file that causes the client to delete the ICA file once it has been used.

Tampering with Configuration Files

The configuration file of the Web Interface may be targeted by an attacker who hopes to modify the configuration of the Web Interface. For example, an attacker may attempt to enable the HTTP version of the HTTPS site (thereby allowing a network sniffer to collect user passwords) or disable two-factor authentication.

Countermeasures

Countermeasures against tampering of configuration files include

▼   Restricting access

▲   Using audit trails

Restricting access can be achieved by limiting the number of users who can log in to the Web Interface server. Audit trails can be used to track which users have modified specific settings. Web Interface administrators should have the following ACL permissions to the configuration files:

▼   Modify

■   Read & Execute

■   List Folder Contents

■   Read

▲   Write

The account under which Web Interface runs requires

▼   Read & Execute

■   List Folder Contents

▲   Read

Setting these ACLs limits the number of individuals who can modify the configuration file and limits the amount of damage any single individual can do.

Profiling

Profiling is an exploratory process that is used to gather information about specific networks. An attacker uses this information to attack known weak points. It is common for web vulnerability scanners to probe web servers for well-known URLs such as FrontPage extensions and other unnecessary Internet Information Services extensions. For a Web Interface, there are two main types of threats from profiling: threats that affect websites and threats that affect network resources.

Common flaws that make servers susceptible to profiling include

▼ Unnecessary services

■ Open ports

▲ Web servers that provide configuration information in their headers

Common techniques used for profiling include

▼ Port scans

■ Ping sweeps

▲ Network Basic Input/Output System (NETBIOS) and Server Message Block (SMB) enumeration

Countermeasures

Countermeasures against Web-based threats include blocking Web robots and limiting configuration information in HTTP headers.

Countermeasures against network-based threats include blocking all unnecessary ports, blocking Internet Control Message Protocol (ICMP) traffic, and disabling unnecessary protocols such as NETBIOS and SMB.

The Windows 2003 Security Configuration Wizard is a useful tool that enables a system administrator to control services, ports, and the like, on the server. Refer to "Secure the Operating System" later in this chapter for further details.

Worms, Viruses, and Other Malicious Software

Malicious software on the Web Interface can disrupt the availability of the Web Interface's services and pose a threat to other machines in the DMZ and the intranet.

Countermeasures

Countermeasures against malicious software include

▼ Protective network-based hardware

■ Protective network-based software

■ Protective host-based software

▲ Limiting the exposure of the Web Interface

Protective network-based hardware such as a firewall helps prevent unauthorized communication with the Web Interface. Some protective network-based software, such as intrusion prevention systems, attempts to prevent attack traffic from reaching hosts. Intrusion detection systems monitor for suspicious activity and can be network-based, host-based, or both. Similarly, host-based software such as antivirus software and anti-spyware software helps prevent malicious software from damaging the server. To limit the exposure of the Web Interface, do not run software such as Web browsers or instant messaging clients on the Web Interface server.

Whenever possible, it is advisable to use a dedicated Web Interface server. A dedicated Web Interface server has several security benefits over a Web Interface server that runs on the same machine as other Citrix products and incurs only the cost of one extra machine. Since they are running fewer applications, dedicated Web Interface servers have a smaller attack surface and can be protected more tightly by firewalls and access restrictions. Additionally, if a dedicated server is compromised or fails, other servers may not be affected.

STEPS FOR SECURING WEB INTERFACE SERVER

The following steps to secure the Web Interface server are discussed below:

▼   Secure the operating system.

■   Restrict access to the Web Interface server.

■   Configure authentication.

■   Secure the link between the Web Interface and the Presentation Server.

■   Secure the link between the Web Interface and the Secure Gateway.

■   Secure the Web Interface for use with the Program Neighborhood Agent.

■   Protect the log files.

▲   Configure auditing.

Secure the Operating System

Windows

This section discusses some procedures necessary to secure the operating system. It covers the following topics, which must be completed in the order listed:

▼   Windows Server 2003 Security Configuration Wizard

▲   Windows Group Policy

NOTE   After completing these steps, administrators still have to follow their regular procedures for securing a server.

Enable HTTPS-Only for IIS   To enable HTTPS-only access to Internet Information Server (IIS), open the Internet Information Services Manager found at **Start > Program Files > Administrator Tools**:

1. Under **Internet Information Services**, expand the tree until the **Default Website** is visible.

2. Right click on the **Default Website** and select **Properties**.

3. Select the **Directory Security** tab.

4. In the **Secure Communications** section, click **Edit**.

5. Click the **Require Secure Channel** box and **Require 128-bit Encryption** and click **OK**.

6. Click **OK**.

Security Configuration Wizard   The Windows 2003 Security Configuration Wizard allows administrators to secure their servers. It provides a mechanism to lock down the ports used by various services and disable Windows services that are unnecessary for a particular server. The options that appear when one is running the Windows Server 2003 Security Configuration Wizard vary with the choices made by the administrator.

NOTE Administrators may have to modify these steps to account for installed applications such as antivirus software and firewalls.

To install and run the Security Configuration Wizard, do the following:

1. Log on to the server as a Windows administrator.

2. Launch the Add or Remove Programs tool (**Start > Control Panel > Add or Remove Programs**).

3. Click **Add/Remove Windows Components** to bring up the **Windows Components Wizard**.

4. Select the **Security Configuration Wizard** check box and click **Next**. A number of progress messages temporarily appear.

5. When the installation is complete, click **Finish**.

6. Close the **Add or Remove Programs** dialog box.

7. Launch the Security Configuration Wizard (**Start > Administrative Tools > Security Configuration Wizard**).

8. At the **Welcome** screen, click **Next**.

9. At the **Configuration Action** screen, select **Create a new security policy** and click **Next**.

10. At the **Select Server** screen, leave the default value and click **Next**.

11. At the **Processing Security Configuration Database** screen, wait for the system scan to complete and click **Next**.

12. At the **Role-Based Service Configuration** screen, click **Next**.

13. The options administrators should select from the **Select Server Roles** screen vary with the machine to which they are applying the Security Configuration Wizard. Each of the subsequent screens requires selection from the different options listed in Table 5-1.

Screen	Options
Select Server Roles	
Select Client Features	DNS Client*, DNS Registration Client*, Domain Member*, Microsoft Networking Client.
	*Required only if the Web Interface server is part of a domain.
Select Administration and Other Options	IPsec Services*, Windows Firewall.
	*Only if IPsec is in use on the Web Interface server.
Select Additional Services	N/A
Handling Unspecified Services	Do not change the start-up mode of the service.
Confirm Service Changes	Click **Next**.
Network Security	Leave **Skip this section** unchecked and click **Next**.
Open Ports and Approved Applications	443 (HTTPS).
Confirm Port Configuration	Click **Next**.
Registry Settings	Leave **Skip this section** unchecked and click **Next**.
Require Server Message Block (SMB) Security Signatures	Uncheck **All computers that connect to satisfy the following operating system requirements** and **It has surplus processor capacity that can be used to sign file and print traffic**.
	Click **Next**.
Outbound Authentication Methods	Domain accounts.
Outbound Authentication Using Domain Accounts	Windows NT 4.0 SP6 or later operating systems.
Inbound Authentication Methods	N/A
Registry Settings Summary	Click **Next**.

(continued on next page)

Table 5-1. Recommended Security Configuration Settings

Screen	Options
Audit Policy	Check the **Skip this section** box and click **Next**.
Internet Information Services	Leave this section cleared. Click **Next**.
Select Web Services for Dynamic Content	**ASP.NET**. Prohibit all other Web Service extensions not listed above.
Select the Virtual Directories to Retain	None selected.
Prevent Anonymous Users from Accessing Content Files	Check **Deny anonymous users write access to content files**.
IIS Settings Summary	Click **Next**.

Table 5-1. Recommended Security Configuration Settings (continued)

14. On the **Save Security Policy** screen, click **Next**.

15. On the **Security Policy File Name** screen, type an appropriate name in the **Security policy** file name box and click **Next**.

16. In the dialog box that appears suggesting that a server restart is required, click **OK**.

17. On the **Apply Security Policy** screen, select **Apply Now** and click **Next**. An **Applying Security Policy** screen appears while the security policy is applied. This may take up to 2 minutes to complete.

18. On the **Applying Security Policy** screen, click **Next**.

19. On the **Completing the Security Configuration Wizard** screen, click **Finish**.

20. Restart the Web Interface server for the new security policies to take effect.

Configure Windows Group Policy   If the Web Interface server is not part of an active directory domain, set security options in security policies to match the organization's security policy. Local policies can be changed by using the MMC.

1. Log on to the domain controller as a domain administrator and start the MMC (**Start > Run** type **mmc** and click **OK**). The **Console1** window appears.

2. From the File menu, click **Add/Remove Snap-in**. At the **Add/Remove Snapin** dialog box, click **Add**. Select **Group Policy Object Editor** and click **Add**.

3. The **Select Group Policy Object** dialog box is set to **Local Computer**.

4. Click **Finish**, then click **OK**.

The following local machine policies also can be configured in the **Computer Configuration** panel. These policy settings should be configured in accordance with the organization's internal policies.

▼ Password

■ Account Lockout

■ Event Log

■ Internet Explorer

■ Remote Assistance

▲ Internet Communication Management

Unix/Linux

When running the Web Interface on a Unix or Linux server, follow these general guidelines:

▼ Do not install the X Window System.

■ Install only the services required to run the Web Interface.

■ Disable unused network daemons such as Network File System (NFS).

■ Disable unsecure remote access tools such as rlogin, rexec, rcp, and rsh (including for the root user).

■ Disable logon by root, including at the console.

■ Create a group for performing privileged functions.

■ Create an administrator account and do not use the root for day-to-day tasks. Add the administrator to the group created above.

■ Keep security patches up to date.

▲ Consider using another server as a loghost server.

Disable Search Engine Robots

To prevent attackers from using search engines or Web crawlers, which also are known as robots, to find Web Interface deployments, administrators should create a robots.txt file in the root of the website. The file should be a plain text file and should contain these two lines:

```
User-agent: *
Disallow: /
```

This tells the robot that it is not allowed to access any part of the site. In addition, some modern robots also follow rules added to the home page of the Web server. The following HTML META tag is used:

```
<META NAME="ROBOTS" CONTENT="NOINDEX">
```

A well-behaved robot such as those used by major search engines will honor this command, but not all robots are well behaved, and some may ignore this file.

Restrict Access to Web Interface Server

To protect the Web Interface, it is important to limit who has access to administrative functions. There are two places where a person can access administrative functions: over the network and locally at the server.

Limit Network Access to Web Interface

As shown in the figures earlier in the chapter, in certain deployments, anyone on the Internet can send traffic to the Web Interface. The Web Interface can communicate with clients on ports 80 (HTTP) and 443 (HTTPS). A firewall must be in place between the Internet and the Web Interface to block all other traffic. Similarly, administrators are advised to place a firewall between the Web Interface and the intranet to form a DMZ. By using a DMZ, the administrator can limit the damage if the Web Interface server becomes compromised. Refer to Figures 5-1A and B for further information.

For an Internet-accessible deployment of the Web Interface, the Secure Gateway provides an increased level of security, decreasing risk to the Web Interface server. Refer to Chapter 4, "Secure Gateway," for further information.

The Web Interface Should Be in a Workgroup

Unless there is a specific requirement for the Web Interface server to be part of a domain, the Web Interface server should be operated as a member of a workgroup. This limits the number of accounts, prevents domain accounts from being compromised if the Web Interface server becomes compromised, and allows stronger and more secure policies to be run locally.

Configure Secure Communication

Refer to the earlier section "Enable HTTPS Only for IIS" to configure secure communication from the client to the Web Interface server.

Configure Authentication

Configure Two-Factor Authentication

1. Open the Access Suite Console and go to the Web Interface site.
2. In the **Common Tasks** panel, select **Configure authentication methods**.
3. In the **Configure authentication methods** window, check **Explicit**.

4. To enable two-factor authentication, highlight **Explicit**.

5. In the **Explicit methods settings**, select the required two-factor authentication method.

6. Click **Next**.

7. Click **Next**.

8. Click **Finish**.

Configure Smart Card Authentication

1. Open the Access Suite Console and go to the Web Interface site.

2. In the **Common Tasks** panel, select **Configure authentication methods**.

3. In the **Configure authentication methods** window, check **Smartcard**.

4. Click **Finish**.

5. Launch the IIS Manager (**Start > Programs > Administrative Tools > Internet Information Services (IIS) Manager**).

6. Right click on the Web Sites directory located under the server running the Web Interface and click **Properties**.

7. From the **Directory Security** tab, select **Enable the Windows directory service mapper** in the **Secure Communications** section.

8. Click **OK** to enable the Directory Service Mapper.

NOTE The Windows Directory Service Mapper requires that the Web Interface server is a member of the Active Directory domain forest.

Secure Link between Web Interface and Presentation Server

Consult the section on secure communication in Chapter 2, "Secure Deployments," for further information about SSL, TLS, and IPsec. This section deals with SSL and TLS connections between the Web Interface server and the Presentation Server.

Secure Web Interface on Windows

Securing the Web Interface on Windows to the Presentation Server requires the use of SSL/TLS. Using SSL/TLS requires root and server certificates. Refer to Appendix D, "SSl/TLS Certificate Installation," for further information.

Enable SSL/TLS to the Presentation Server

To use encryption between the Web Interface and the Presentation Server, perform the steps described in the following lists.

Using the Access Suite Console:

1. Open the Access Suite Console and go to the Web Interface site.

2. In the **Common Tasks** panel, select **Manage Server Farms**.

3. Double left click on the farm on which the settings are to be changed.

4. Set the **Transport Type** to **SSL Relay**.

5. Click **OK**.

6. Click **OK**.

Directly editing webinterface.conf:

1. Open the webinterface.conf file.

2. Change the **SSLRelayPort** setting in the **Farm<*n*>** parameter to the port number of the Citrix SSL Relay on the server.

3. Change the value of the **Transport** setting in the **Farm<n>** parameter to **SSL**.

4. Save and close the webinterface.conf file.

5. Restart the Web server to apply the changes.

Securing Web Interface on Unix/Linux

This section assumes that the Web Interface is properly configured to run under Unix and is working. The Web Interface on Unix/Linux runs in the Tomcat Web application server. To secure Tomcat, the following configuration changes can be made:

1. Open the server.xml file in the Tomcat configuration directory.

2. Look for **SSL HTTP/1.1** and set the port to listen on 443.

3. Remove all unwanted and sample Web applications from the "webapps" directory in the Tomcat installation directory.

4. To disable directory listings, edit the conf/web.xml file in the Tomcat installation directory and set the listings to **false** in the default servlet settings.

5. Restart Tomcat for the changes to take effect.

Refer to Appendix D, "SSl/TLS Certificate Installation," for further information on certificates.

Secure Link between Web Interface and Secure Gateway

Consult the section on secure communication in Chapter 2, "Secure Deployments," for further information on SSL/TLS and IPsec. This section deals with SSL/TLS connections between the Web Interface server and the Secure Gateway server.

Enable SSL/TLS to Secure Gateway   This is configured on the Secure Gateway. Consult Chapter 4, "Secure Gateway," for further details.

Secure Web Interface on Windows

Enable Secure Gateway and STA Tickets

1. Open the Access Suite Console and go to the Web Interface site.

2. In the **Common Tasks** panel, select **Manage secure client access**.

3. From the **Edit Secure Gateway settings** dialog box, specify the Fully Qualified Domain Name (FQDN) of the Secure Gateway server that clients must use in the **Secure Gateway address (FQDN)** field. This must match exactly what was specified in the common name field when the certificate was created.

4. Specify the port number on the Secure Gateway server that clients must use in the Secure Gateway **port** field. The default port number is 443.

5. To use session reliability, select the **Enable Session Reliability through Secure Gateway 3.0** option.

6. In the **Secure Ticket Authorities** area, click **Add** to specify the URL of a Secure Ticket Authority that the Web Interface can use. The STA is displayed in the **Secure Ticket Authority URLs** list. The Secure Ticket Authority is part of the XML service. Its URL will be of the form https://FQDN-of-STA-server/Scripts/CtxStA.dll.

7. Click **OK** to finish making changes.

Secure Web Interface on Unix/Linux

Enable Secure Gateway and STA Tickets   Open the webinterface.conf file and change the following settings:

▼ **CSG_EnableSessionReliability**=On or Off

■ **CSG_Server**=FQDN of CSG server

■ **CSG_ServerPort**=port number

■ **CSG_STA_URL1**=http://fqdn/scripts/CtxSTA.dll or

■ **CSG_STA_URL1**=https://fqdn/scripts/CtxSTA.dll for a secure link

▲ **ClientAddressMap**=*,SG

Save the changes and restart the Web server for the changes to take effect.

Secure Web Interface for Use with Program Neighborhood Agent

To secure the connection between the Program Neighborhood Agent site and the Presentation Server, enable SSL. This can be performed by using the Access Suite Console.

Enable SSL/TLS to Presentation Server

To use encryption between the Web Interface Program Neighborhood Agent Site and the Presentation Server, do the following.

Enable SSL/TLS to Presentation Server by Using Access Suite Console

1. Open the Access Suite Console and go to the Program Neighborhood Agent site.
2. In the **Common Tasks** panel, select **Manage Server Farms**.
3. Double left click on the farm on which the settings are to be changed.
4. Set the **Transport Type** to **SSL Relay**.
5. Click **OK**.
6. Click **OK**.

Enable SSL/TLS to Presentation Server by Directly Editing webinterface.conf File

1. Open the webinterface.conf file.
2. Scroll down to the section containing the configuration information for the PNAgent site.
3. Change the **SSLRelayPort** setting in the **Farm<n>** parameter to the port number of the Citrix SSL Relay on the server.
4. Change the value of the **Transport** setting in the **Farm<n>** parameter to **SSL**.
5. Save and close the webinterface.conf file.
6. Restart the Web server to apply the changes.

To secure the connection between the Program Neighborhood Agent and the Web Interface, enable HTTPS. This can be done by using the ASC.

1. Open the Access Suite Console and go to the Program Neighborhood Agent site.
2. Expand the tree until config.xml is visible.
3. Right click on the config.xml file and select **Edit**.
4. Check the box for "Use SSL/TLS for communication between the client and this site."
5. Click **OK**.

Refer to the section "Configure Program Neighborhood Agent to Use SSL/TLS" in Chapter 8, "Presentation Server Client," for information on how to enable HTTPS for the PNAgent.

Protect Log Files

To help prevent attackers from reading or tampering with log files, administrators should protect log files with proper ACLs and backups. The Web Interface uses the Windows

Application and System Event logs to record events, which, by default on Windows 2003, are accessible only by administrators. Windows Event logs are append-only to prevent modification. However, administrators, or attackers who have gained administrative privileges, can clear the logs. Administrators should ensure that only administrators have **Read** and **List Folder Contents** permissions to the logs directory.

To protect log data from loss, the logs should be backed up regularly. For Unix and Linux systems, set permissions on the system logs to be readable and writable by the root user and readable by any member of the administrators group.

TIP   If possible, run more than one loghost. If a malicious user deletes local logs, there will still be a record of his or her actions.

Configure Auditing

Auditing enables the Web Interface server administrator to perform a security analysis after a system breach. Windows Server 2003 auditing is enabled in using policies. The settings shown next are suggested for a Web Interface server in the absence of any organizational policies on the subject. Existing organizational policies should receive preference over the settings suggested in this chapter.

Enable Security Audit Logging in Windows 2003

1. Log on to the server as a Windows administrator.
2. Launch the Local Security Settings (**Start > Settings > Control Panel > Administrative Tools > Local Security Policy**).
3. Click to expand **Local Policies**.
4. Double click on **Audit Policy**. Table 5-2 contains the typical recommended audit policy settings.
5. Exit the local security settings (**File > Exit**).
6. Reboot the Web Interface server.

VERIFY SECURED CONFIGURATION

To verify that all the security steps have been followed, perform the following actions. Verify that only port 443 is open:

1. Using a port scanner, scan the Web Interface server from within the DMZ.
2. Only port 443 will respond.

Verify that the client to Web Interface connection is encrypted by performing the following steps.

Policy	Description	Security Setting
Audit account logon events	Determines whether an account logon should be recorded in the security log. The event is recorded in both the domain controller and the local security log.	Success, Failure
Audit account management	Determines whether to audit events related to users and groups. Account creation, password updates, and group membership changes all generate unique audit events.	Success, Failure
Audit directory service access	Determines whether to audit events when a user accesses an active directory object with a Systems Access Control List (SACL).	No auditing
Audit logon events	Determines whether an account logon or logoff event should be generated.	Success, Failure
Audit object access	Determines whether access on objects with SACLs should generate audit events.	No auditing
Audit policy change	Determines whether changes to user rights, audit, and trust policies should generate audit events.	Success, Failure
Audit privilege use	Determines whether audit events should be generated when users exercise user rights.	Failure
Audit process tracking	Determines whether audit events for process-related events should be generated. For example, process-related events include process creation, process termination, handle duplication, and primary token assignments.	No auditing
Audit system events	Determines whether audit events should be generated when events that affect the system or security log are generated, such as computer restarts or halts.	Failure

Table 5-2.   Recommended Audit Policy Settings

1. Using a network monitoring tool, start a network capture.
2. From the client, log in to the Web Interface.
3. Stop the network capture and view the results.

4. Filter the results so that only traffic between the client and the Web Interface server is displayed.

5. Confirm that all traffic between the client and the Web Interface is encrypted.

6. Confirm that the destination port should be 443 on the Web Interface side.

Verify that the connection from the client to the Web Interface Program Neighborhood Agent is encrypted:

1. Using a network monitoring tool, start a network capture.

2. From the client, right click on the PNAgent icon and add the HTTPS address of the Web Interface PNAgent site.

3. From the client, right click on the PNAgent icon and select refresh.

4. Check that the published application is visible in the **Start > Programs** menu.

5. Stop the network capture and view the results.

6. Filter the results so that only traffic between the client and the Web Interface server is displayed.

7. Confirm that all traffic between the client and the Web Interface is encrypted.

8. Confirm that the destination port is 443.

Verify that the Web Interface Presentation Server and the Program Neighborhood Agent to Presentation Server connections are encrypted:

1. Using a network monitoring tool, start a network capture.

2. From the client, log in to the Web Interface.

3. At the network monitor, stop the network capture and view the results.

4. Filter the results so that only traffic between the Web Interface and the Presentation Server is displayed.

5. Confirm that all traffic between the Web Interface and the Presentation Server is encrypted.

6. Confirm that the destination port is 443.

Verify that the connection from the Web Interface to the Secure Gateway is encrypted:

1. Using a network monitoring tool, start a network capture.

2. From the client, log in to the Web Interface.

3. At the network monitor, stop the network capture and view the results.

4. Filter the results so that only traffic between the Web Interface and the Secure Gateway is displayed.

5. Confirm that all traffic between the Web Interface and the Secure Gateway is encrypted.

6. Confirm that the destination port is 443.

Verify ACL permissions for the webinterface.conf file:

1. Create a non-administrator user.
2. Log in as the created user to the Web Interface server.
3. Open the webinterface.conf file and make some changes.
4. Try to save the file.
5. Confirm that it is not possible for the user to make changes to the webinterface .conf.

Verify that the audit logs are correctly configured:

1. Log in to the Web Interface server as the created user.
2. Log out.
3. Log in to the Web Interface server as the administrator.
4. Open the Event Viewer, go to the Security log, and check that both the administrator and non-administrator users' login/logouts are listed.
5. Remove the account of the non-administrator user.

Verify that ticketing is enabled:

1. From the client, log in to the Web Interface.
2. Right click on an application and save the ICA file to the desktop.
3. Right click the saved ICA file and select "Open With…".
4. Select "Notepad."
5. The contents of the ICA file are displayed.
6. The FQDN or IP:port of the Presentation Server is not displayed on the **Address=** line.
7. Finally, close the ICA file, wait approximately 3 minutes (assuming the ticket time to live is at the default 100 seconds), and attempt to launch the application.
8. The application launch will fail with "Cannot connect to the Citrix MetaFrame server. The Citrix SSL server you have selected is not accepting connections."

SUMMARY

This chapter explored threats to the Citrix Web Interface, countermeasures to each of those threats, and ways to implement each countermeasure. Always keep the operating system, antivirus software, and Web Interface up to date with the latest security patches, hot fixes, and service packs.

CHAPTER 6

Password Manager

This chapter explains how to protect the Citrix Password Manager. The discussion covers the assets of the Password Manager, threats to those assets, countermeasures to the threats, and instructions for implementing the countermeasures in a Password Manager environment.

DEPLOYMENTS

Administrators can deploy the Password Manager in several different ways. A stand-alone deployment is a deployment that is independent of other Citrix products. This type of deployment can use a central store that is either an NTFS network share (Figure 6-1) or an Active Directory container (Figure 6-2).

Another deployment option is to deploy the Password Manager as a hosted application on the Citrix Presentation Server. When this is done, the Password Manager Agent is deployed in conjunction with a published application. As a result, the end user will be able to access only secondary credentials for published applications running in the environment hosted by the Presentation Server. The term *secondary credentials* refers to the entire set of information the user provides to gain access to an application or network resource, including the user ID, the password, and two other configurable fields. These deployments also can use a central store that is either an NTFS network share (Figure 6-3) or an Active Directory container (Figure 6-4).

> **NOTE**   The ICA connections in Figures 6-3 and 6-4 are shown with session reliability enabled on the Presentation Server. If this feature is disabled, port 1494 will be used.

COMPONENTS

The Password Manager is a single sign-on solution that allows users to authenticate only once with a single primary password or smart card, and manages a user's secondary credentials to access Windows-, Web-, and host-based applications.

Password Manager Agent

The Password Manager Agent acts on behalf of the end user, detecting and reacting automatically to password-related events. When a user attempts to access an application that requires authentication, the agent software detects the application's request for authentication, retrieves the correct logon credentials from its local cache, and supplies them to the application. The agent software synchronizes its local cache with the central store each time a new session is started during credential synchronization. This allows users to maintain their credentials and settings from any workstation. Administrators can enter user credentials at configuration time, allowing the agent software to perform all logon and password changes initiated by those applications for an individual user.

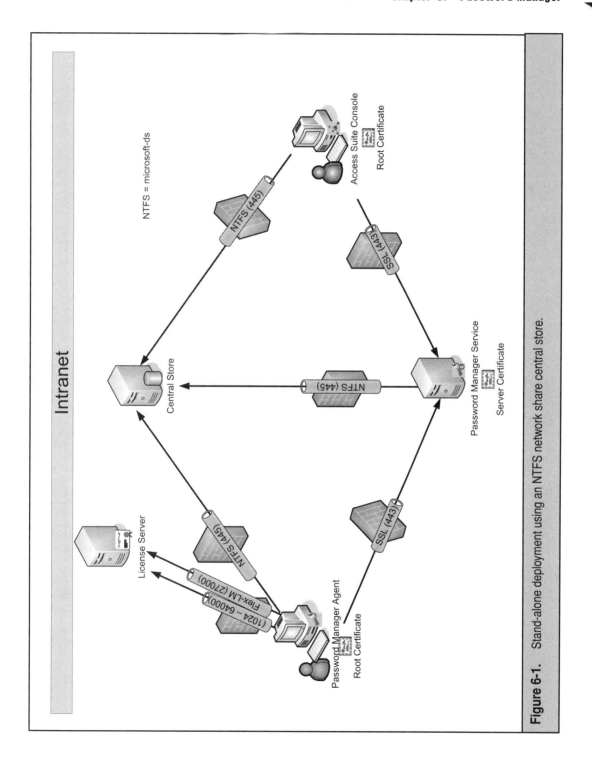

Figure 6-1.   Stand-alone deployment using an NTFS network share central store.

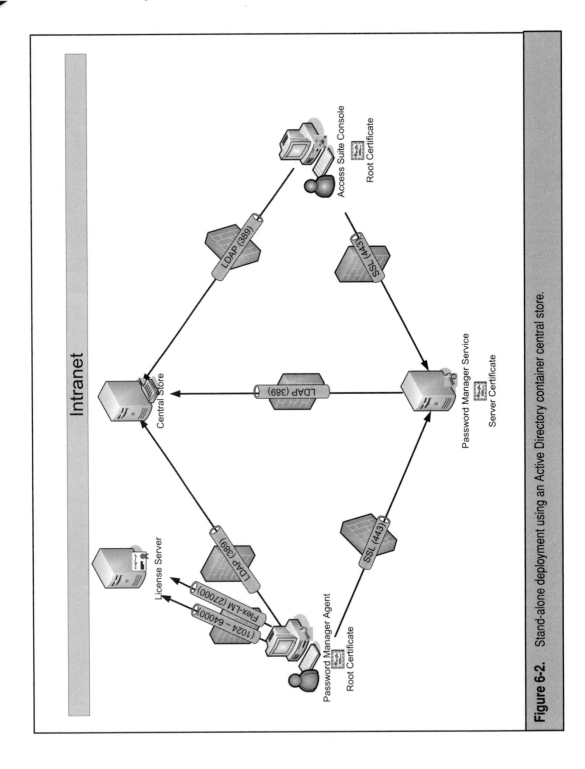

Figure 6-2.   Stand-alone deployment using an Active Directory container central store.

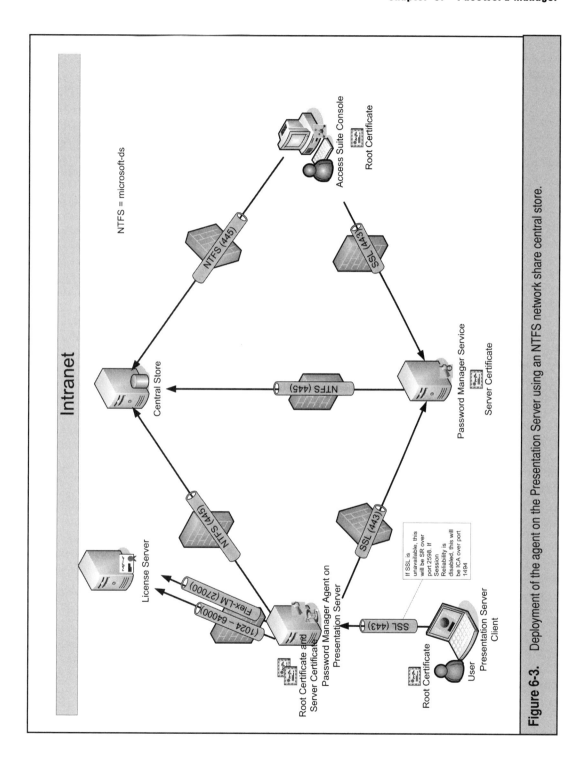

Figure 6-3.   Deployment of the agent on the Presentation Server using an NTFS network share central store.

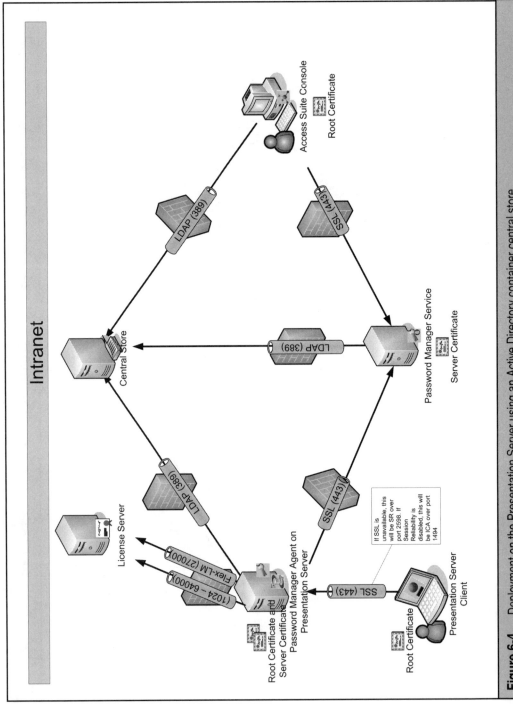

Figure 6-4. Deployment on the Presentation Server using an Active Directory container central store.

Central Store

All users' encrypted credentials are saved in the central store, which is deployed as shared network folders or integrated into Microsoft Active Directory. The central store is divided into two areas: the synchronization area and the administrative data area. Each area contains different types of information and therefore is protected by different ACLs. The synchronization area is a location that the Password Manager Agent contacts to obtain settings and encrypted secondary user credentials. This area is accessible by both administrators and users. The administrative data area is the location where the console stores the administrative configurations that are used to create the Password Manager Agent settings for the users. This area is protected by an ACL that allows access only to administrators. The administrative data in this area include the following:

▼ *Application definitions.* These definitions define the applications for which the Password Manager will maintain password information.

■ *Password policies.* These policies define password complexity requirements for users.

▲ *Security questions.* These are administrator-defined questions that can be employed by a user to verify his or her identity to the Password Manager.

Password Manager Console

The console provides administrators with control over all aspects of password management without giving an administrator the ability to view users' passwords. Using the console, an administrator can configure individual applications for single sign-on, define password policy settings, automate Password Manager Agent interactions, and configure Password Manager Agent settings on the central store. Password policy settings include

▼ Password complexity

■ Password history enforcement

▲ Password expiration warnings

Password Manager Service

The Password Manager Service is a Web service with the following components:

▼ Key Management Module

■ Provisioning Module

▲ Data Integrity Module

The *Key Management Module* allows for the recovery of cryptographic keys used by the Password Manager Agent. If a user's primary authentication credentials change, for instance, if the administrator resets a user's password, the Password Manager Service can perform a cryptographic key recovery to prevent the loss of the user's secondary credentials. Administrators can choose to enforce identity verification, which requires users to provide proof of their identity before recovering their cryptographic keys. Users can verify their identity to the Password Manager by answering security questions established by their administrator or by submitting their previous passwords.

The *Provisioning Module* allows administrators to preset passwords for all Password Manager–configured applications. This eliminates the need for users to know their passwords, reducing the risk of users accidentally disclosing or sharing their passwords.

The *Data Integrity Module* allows administrators to configure the Password Manager to digitally sign all administrative data in the central store. This allows the agent software to verify the integrity of the administrative data downloaded during credential synchronization.

Each of these modules uses cryptographic keys that must remain consistent across servers that host the Password Manager Service. When one is deploying the Password Manager Service on more than one server, these keys must be exported to a file and installed on each new Password Manager Service machine. Collectively, the cryptographic keys and variables used by modules of the service are called the *service data*. Service data include

▼ Key Management Module cryptographic variables

■ The signature key used by the Data Integrity Module

▲ The encryption key used by the Provisioning Module

Password Manager Application Definition Tool

The Password Manager Application Definition Tool is a utility that allows administrators to create application definitions for Windows-, Web-, and host-based applications. This tool can be stand-alone or used from within the console. For the rest of this chapter, the Application Definition Tool will be considered part of the console.

ASSETS

The Citrix Password Manager Agent has the following assets:

▼ *Administrative data.* The security characteristics of this asset are integrity and availability.

■ *Secondary credentials.* The security characteristics of this asset are confidentiality, integrity, and availability.

▲ *Registry keys/values.* The security characteristics of this asset are confidentiality and integrity.

The Citrix Password Manager central store has the following assets:

▼ *Secondary credentials.* The security characteristics of this asset are confidentiality, integrity, and availability.

▲   *Administrative data.* The security characteristics of this asset are integrity and
      availability.

The Citrix Password Manager Service has the following assets:

▼   *Data Integrity Signing Key.* The security characteristics of this asset are confiden-
      tiality and integrity.

■   *Password Manager Service data.* The security characteristics of this asset are confi-
      dentiality, integrity, and availability.

▲   *Secondary credentials.* The security characteristics of this asset are confidentiality,
      integrity, and availability.

THREATS AND COUNTERMEASURES

On the basis of the security principles of each asset described above, the main threats to
the Password Manager are as follows:

▼   Tampering with administrative data on the Password Manager Agent

■   Disclosure of secondary credentials to attackers

■   Disclosure of secondary credentials to users

■   Tampering with administrative data in transit

■   Tampering with secondary credentials in transit

■   Disclosure of secondary credentials on the central store

■   Tampering with secondary credentials on the central store

■   Disclosure of secondary credentials in transit

■   Disclosure of Password Manager Service data

▲   Service disruption

Tampering with Administrative Data
on Password Manager Agent

The Password Manager Console controls the configuration and behavior of the Password Manager Agent by using administrative data. These data are downloaded and
stored by the agent software during synchronization with the central store and stored on
the Password Manager Agent in the form of configuration settings.

Countermeasures

If an attacker is able to compromise the administrative data, the agent software can be
misconfigured to behave in a manner inconsistent with an organization's security policy.

Countermeasures against tampering with administrative data on the Password Manager Agent include the following:

▼ Set appropriate ACLs on registry entries and files.

▲ Configure the agent software to delete the user's data folder and registry keys upon shutdown.

Disclosure of Secondary Credentials to Attackers

Secondary credentials are the main asset the Password Manager protects. On the Password Manager Agent, those credentials are synchronized with the central store and stored in the Local Host Cache.

Countermeasures

No additional configuration is required to protect secondary credentials from disclosure to an attacker. Each set of credentials stored in the Local Host Cache is encrypted using a TripleDES algorithm with a 192-bit key.

Disclosure of Secondary Credentials to Users

Although secondary credentials are protected from disclosure to attackers by encryption, administrators may choose to configure the Password Manager to protect secondary credentials from users. Users often choose easily predictable passwords, log in to company resources from unsecured computers, or give their credentials to other users. These activities can reduce the security of an organization's information systems.

Countermeasures

Countermeasures to the disclosure of secondary credentials include the following:

▼ Create a password policy for all users that includes automatic password changing.

▲ Prevent users from revealing their passwords.

With these countermeasures in place, users are less likely to know their passwords or be able to share them with other users. This prevents unauthorized activity and access to sensitive information from unapproved computers.

Tampering with Administrative Data in Transit

Administrative data created using the Password Manager Console first are transmitted to the central store. When the agent software synchronizes with the central store, the data are transferred to the Password Manager Agent and define the agent software's configuration settings.

Countermeasures

The Data Integrity Module digitally signs all administrative data before the console places the data into the central store. When the agent software synchronizes its administrative data with the central store, the agent software verifies the digital signature on the settings to verify the authenticity and integrity of the downloaded information.

A countermeasure to tampering with administrative data in transit is to enable the Data Integrity Module.

Tampering with Secondary Credentials in Transit

Secondary credentials are transmitted from the Password Manager Console to the Password Manager Service and then to the central store during credential provisioning. They also are transmitted between the central store and the Password Manager Agent during synchronization.

Countermeasures

Countermeasures to tampering with secondary credentials include

- ▼   SSL/TLS connections
- ▲   TripleDES encryption

The Password Manager has built-in security in the form of SSL/TLS connections between the Password Manager Agent and the Password Manager Service and between the Password Manager Console and the Password Manager Service. Furthermore, all credentials transmitted between the central store and the agent software are encrypted with TripleDES encryption. If these data are modified, they become unusable. This mitigates the threat of an attacker changing a password in transit to a usable value. No additional configuration is required to enable these secure connections. Consult Appendix D, "SSL/TLS Certificate Installation," for instructions for installing a digital certificate for SSL/TLS.

Disclosure of Secondary Credentials on Central Store

If attackers gain access to the encrypted credentials on the central store, they can attempt to run a brute force attack to guess the encryption key and thus access the credentials.

Countermeasures

Secondary credentials on the central store are all encrypted with TripleDES encryption, using a 192-bit key to prevent disclosure; however, an administrator can take additional precautions to prevent compromise of the encrypted credentials. Countermeasures to disclosure of secondary credentials include the following:

- ▼   Set appropriate ACLs on the central store folders (if using an NTFS network share).
- ▲   Disable administrative shares on the central store machine.

On Microsoft Windows, several shared network folders are enabled by default. These folders are called administrative shares. Examples of these shares are C$ and ADMIN$. These shares provide unnecessary points of entry to the central store.

Tampering with Secondary Credentials on Central Store

The central store is the main repository for secondary credential information. If an attacker modifies these data, it can result in unauthorized access to a user's configured applications or a service disruption. If the encrypted secondary credentials are corrupted, the decryption of these credentials by a legitimate user will fail. In environments that automatically change passwords and do not disclose credentials to end users, this results in a user being unable to log in to an application.

Countermeasures

Administrators must configure the Password Manager to prevent unauthorized access to the encrypted credentials. Countermeasures to tampering with secondary credentials include the following:

▼ Set appropriate ACLs on central store folders (for NTFS network share central stores).

▲ Set appropriate permissions on Active Directory schemas (for Active Directory central stores).

Disclosure of Password Manager Service Data

In an environment that utilizes more than one machine running the Citrix Password Manager Service, administrators must maintain consistency of the service data across machines. Service data vary on the basis of which features of the service are enabled but can consist of a key variable used by the Key Management Module, the Data Integrity Module's signing key, and a cryptographic key used by the Provisioning Module.

To maintain parity across machines, the administrator must use the Move Service Data Tool to export service data and transfer the data to all servers running the Password Manager Service. Administrators must take proper steps to secure the data both in transit and in storage. A secure method of transporting the data is to export the data to physical media and manually transport them to each additional machine running the Password Manager Service. When the transfer is complete, administrators should destroy the media or store the media in accordance with the physical security policy of their organization.

Countermeasures

Although the Key Management Module uses a split-key encryption system and these data are only one variable used in creating the key, administrators still must take care to prevent the disclosure of the data to an attacker.

If the Data Integrity signing key is compromised, an attacker can gain the ability to sign false configuration settings and pass those settings to the Password Manager Agent.

The false settings will be trusted by the agent software and implemented, potentially reducing the overall security of the system.

If administrators use the Provisioning Module, they must protect the provisioning key. This key may give an attacker access to administrator-provisioned secondary credentials.

The countermeasures to disclosure of Password Manager Service data are as follows:

▼   Choose a strong password to protect the data.

■   Export the file to removable media and store it securely.

▲   Use TripleDES Encryption.

NOTE The encryption is performed automatically by the Password Manager and cannot be configured. No additional steps are required for administrators to enable this feature, and the feature cannot be disabled.

Disclosure of Secondary Credentials in Transit

Secondary credentials are transmitted between the central store and the Password Manager Agent during synchronization. They also are transmitted from the Password Manager Console to the Password Manager Service and then from the service to the central store during credential provisioning. The following countermeasures help prevent the unauthorized modification of secondary credentials in transit.

Countermeasures

Countermeasures to disclosure of secondary credentials include

▼   SSL/TLS connections

▲   TripleDES encryption

The Password Manager has built-in security in the form of an SSL/TLS connection between the Password Manager Console and the Password Manager Service. No additional configuration is required to enable these secure connections. All credentials transmitted between the agent software and the central store are encrypted with TripleDES encryption. If these credentials are modified in transit, they become unusable. This prevents attackers from modifying the credentials in a way that would give them unauthorized access.

Service Disruption

Service disruptions must be planned for. They can be caused by nonmalicious or malicious activity. Causes of service disruptions include the reasons described in the following list.

▼ *System failure*
- Software failures
- Hardware failures
- Power failures

■ *Human error*
- Accidental deletion of files
- Misconfiguration

▲ *Malicious behavior*
- Denial-of-service attacks

Countermeasures

Countermeasures to nonmalicious service disruptions include the following:

▼ Restrict access to Password Manager administration functions.

▲ Back up important files.

Countermeasures to denial-of-service attacks include enabling logging of Password Manager events.

Restricting access permissions for users on the Password Manager Console limits the damage that any single person can do. Backups allow for recovery from service disruptions and malicious software. Proper logging provides a mechanism for recognizing an attack and identifying any authenticated users who may be involved.

STEPS FOR SECURING PASSWORD MANAGER AGENT

The following steps for securing the Password Manager Agent are discussed below:

▼ Configure the Password Manager Agent with smart cards.

■ Create a secure user configuration.

■ Configure the secure user configuration.

▲ Create a secure password policy.

Configure Password Manager with Smart Cards

Users can authenticate to the Password Manager with smart cards. In an environment utilizing this method of authentication, follow these steps.

NOTE   For a detailed discussion of smart cards, refer to Chapter 2, "Secure Deployments."

1. Log on to the Password Manager Console.
2. Navigate to **Citrix Access Suite Console > Suite Components > Password Manager > User Configurations**.
3. Select the user configuration to edit from the drop-down menu.
4. Click **Edit User Configuration**.
5. Select **Client-side Interaction** from the menu on the left.
6. Under **Smart Card key source**, choose **Smart Card Data Protect**.
7. Click **OK**.

Create Secure User Configuration

All Password Manager Agent security is configured through options set in the Password Manager Console. When creating new user configurations, administrators should apply certain settings to maintain maximum security, as shown in Table 6-1.

Screen	Options
User Configuration Description	Fill in the **Name**, **Description**, and **User administrative data location** fields and click **Next**.
Choose Policies and Applications	Choose application groups to include in this configuration.
	Click **Next**.
Configure Agent Interaction	Ensure that only **Submit application credentials automatically** is checked.
	Change **Time between agent re-authentication requests** to 2 hours.
Configure Licensing	Fill in the license server address.
	Select the appropriate licensing model.
	Click **Next**.
Synchronization	Ensure that only **Notify user when agent synchronization fails** is checked.
	Click **Next**.

(continued on next page)

Table 6-1.   Creating a Secure User Configuration

Screen	Options
Configure Key Management	Key recovery method: If users should not be prompted for identity verification, select **Retrieve Key automatically;** do not prompt the user to verify his or her identity. If users should be prompted for identity verification, select **Prompt user to select the method: previous password or security questions**. (For instructions on installing and configuring the Key Management Module, consult the Password Manager Administrator Guide.) **NOTE** *In environments where administrators* must *not have access to user application passwords, users* must *be prompted for identity verification.* Click **Next**.
Enable Self-Service Features	Ensure that all check boxes are cleared. Click **Next**.
Key Management Module	Fill in the **URL** field with the location of the Password Manager Service. Ensure that the **service port** is **443**. Click **Next**.
Provisioning Module	Click **Next**.
Confirm Settings	Verify that the settings are correct. Click **Finish**.

Table 6-1. Creating a Secure User Configuration (continued)

Configure Secure User Configuration

After administrators create a user configuration, they should edit that configuration to enable additional security features. The settings outlined in this section do not allow users to configure the Password Manager to authenticate to personal applications and prevent users from viewing their own passwords. This setup requires administrators to preconfigure all applications for which a user should have passwords. Only applications configured by an administrator will be recognized by the Password Manager when this user configuration is employed. Fields marked N/A in Table 6-2 have no security implications or do not require the attention of the administrator for this configuration.

To give users the ability to define their own applications in the Password Manager, administrators must make a few changes to the preceding instructions. Those changes occur in the "Basic Agent Interaction" and "Client side Interaction" sections, as shown in Table 6-3.

Screen	Options
User Configuration Description	N/A
Basic Agent Interaction	Ensure that only **Submit application credentials automatically** is checked.
	Ensure that **Time between agent re-authentication requests** is 2 hours.
Agent User Interface	Ensure that all check boxes are cleared.
Client-side Interaction	Ensure that only **Delete user's data folder and registry keys when the agent is shut down** and **Limit the number of days to keep track of deleted credentials** are checked.
	Ensure that the number of days to keep track of deleted credentials is 180.
	Ensure that the smart card key source is **Smart Card Data Protect**.
Synchronization	Ensure that only **Notify user when agent synchronization fails** is checked.
Application Support	Ensure that **Detect client-side application definitions** is unchecked.
	Ensure that **Number of domain name levels to match** is 99.
Hot Desktop	N/A
Licensing	N/A
Update License	N/A

(continued on next page)

Table 6-2. Modifying the Secure User Configuration

Screen	Options
Key Management	Key recovery method:
	If users should not be prompted for identity verification, select **Retrieve Key automatically;** do not prompt a user to verify his or her identity.
	If users should be prompted for identity verification, select **Prompt user to select the method: previous password or security questions**.
	(For instructions on installing and configuring the Key Management Module, consult the Password Manager Administrator Guide.)
	NOTE In environments where administrators must not have access to user application passwords, users should be prompted for identity verification.
	Click **Next**.
Self-Service Features	Ensure that both check boxes are unchecked.
Key Management Module	Ensure that the **Service port** is **443**.
Provisioning Module	If administrators will not be using the Provisioning Module, ensure that **Use provisioning** is unchecked.

Table 6-2. Modifying the Secure User Configuration (continued)

Screen	Options
Basic Agent Interaction	Check **Automatically detect applications and prompt user to store credentials**.
Client-side Interaction	Check **Enable users to cancel credential storage when a new application is detected**.

Table 6-3. Allowing Users to Store Their Own Credentials

Create Secure Password Policy

A password policy is a group of settings, established by the administrator, that is used to manage Password Manager–configured applications. Password policies can be used to manage character requirements and the length of passwords created or changed by the Password Manager. Administrators should create password policies that adhere to their organization's official password policy. Following is an example of the steps taken to create a password policy that requires uppercase, lowercase, and special characters and has a minimum length of 12 characters. This policy also prevents users from viewing their passwords in the Logon Manager.

1. Log on to the Password Manager Console.
2. Drill down to **Suite Components > Password Manager > Password Policies**.
3. Click **Create new password policy**.

Name password policy	**Enter a name and description**
Set basic password rules	Alphabet case usage: **Allow uppercase and lowercase alphabetic characters**
	Minimum password length: **12**
	Maximum password length: **25**
	Number of times a single character can be repeated: **4**
	Number of times a character can be repeated sequentially: **1**
	Click **Next**.
Set numeric character rules	Ensure that **Allow numeric characters, Password can begin with a numeric character,** and **Password can end with a numeric character** are checked.
	Minimum number of numeric characters required: **1**
	Maximum number of numeric characters allowed: **4**
	Click **Next**.
Set special character rules	Ensure that **Allow special characters, Password can begin with a special character**, and **Password can end with a special character** are checked.
	Minimum number of special characters required: **1**
	Maximum number of special characters allowed: **4**
	Click **Next**.
	(continued on next page)

Table 6-4.   Creating a Secure Password Policy

Name password policy	Enter a name and description
Establish logon preferences	Ensure that **Allow user to reveal password for applications** is unchecked.
	Ensure that **Force user to re-authenticate before submitting application credentials** is checked.
	Number of logon retries: **1**
	Time limit for number of retries: **30**
	Click **Next**.
Set password expiration options	Ensure that **Use the password expiration settings associated with the application definitions** is unchecked.
	Click **Next**.
Define Password Wizard	Agent Password Wizard options: **System-generated, silent**
	Click **Next**.
	Click **Finish**.

Table 6-4.   Creating a Secure Password Policy (continued)

Apply this password policy to all security-sensitive business applications to prevent users from having access to their secondary credentials. This prevents users from accessing applications from noncompany resources and also provides a strong password.

STEPS FOR SECURING PASSWORD MANAGER SERVICE

Follow these steps for securing the Password Manager Service:

▼ Secure the operating system

■ Enable the Data Integrity Module

■ Configure auditing

▲ Secure the Password Manager Service data

Secure the Operating System

The Windows 2003 Security Configuration Wizard allows administrators to secure the operating system. It provides a mechanism to lock down the ports used by various services and disable Windows services that are unnecessary. The options that appear while running the Windows Server 2003 Security Configuration Wizard vary with the choices made along the way.

To Install and Run Security Configuration Wizard

1. Log on to the server as a Windows user with local administrator rights.

2. Launch the Add or Remove Programs tool (**Start > Control Panel > Add or Remove Programs**).

3. Click **Add/Remove Windows Components** to bring up the **Windows Components Wizard**.

4. Select the **Security Configuration Wizard** check box and click **Next**. A number of progress messages temporarily appear.

5. When the installation is complete, click **Finish**.

6. Close the **Add or Remove Programs** dialog box.

7. Launch the Security Configuration Wizard (**Start > Administrative Tools > Security Configuration Wizard**).

8. At the **Welcome** screen, click **Next**.

9. At the **Configuration Action** screen, ensure that **Create a new security policy** is selected and click **Next**.

10. At the **Select Server** screen, leave the default value and click **Next**.

11. At the **Processing Security Administrative Database** screen, wait for the system scan to complete and click **Next**.

12. At the **Role-Based Service Configuration** screen, click **Next**.

13. The options that administrators should select from this screen vary with the machine to which they are applying the Security Configuration Wizard. Each of the subsequent screens requires the selection of different options, as listed in Table 6-5. The N/A (Not Applicable) entries mean that administrators should not select any options or that the screen does not exist.

NOTE Administrators may have to modify these steps to account for installed software such as antivirus software and third-party firewalls.

Screen	Options
Select Server Roles	Web Server
	Middle-Tier Application Server
Select Client Features	Automatic update client
	DHCP client (if server obtains address via DHCP)
	DNS client
	DNS registration client (if server obtains address via DHCP)
	Domain member
	Microsoft networking client
Select Administration and Other Options	Time synchronization
	Windows firewall
Select Additional Services	Citrix XTE Server
	Diagnostic Facility COM Server
Handling Unspecified Services	Do not change the start-up mode of the service.
Confirm Service Changes	Click **Next**.
Network Security	Leave **Skip this section** cleared and click **Next**.
Open Ports and Approved Applications	139 (netbios-ssn)
	443 (HTTPS)
	Ports used by Citrix XTE Server (XTE.exe)
	Ports used by Diagnostic Facility COM Server (CdfSvc.exe)
Confirm Port Configuration	Leave **Skip this section** cleared and click **Next**.
Registry Settings	Leave **Skip this section** cleared and click **Next**.
Require SMB Security Signatures	Leave **All computers that connect to it satisfy the minimum operating system requirements** checked.
	Leave **It has surplus process capacity that can be used to sign the file and print traffic** checked.
	Click **Next**.
Outbound Authentication Methods	Domain accounts

Table 6-5. Security Configuration Wizard

Screen	Options
Outbound Authentication Using Domain Accounts	Windows NT 4.0 Service Pack 6a or later operating systems
Inbound Authentication Methods	N/A
Registry Settings Summary	Click **Next**.
Audit Policy	Leave the **Skip this section** check box cleared and click **Next**.
	Select **Audit successful and unsuccessful activities**.
	Click **Next**.
Internet Information Services	Leave **Skip this section** cleared and click **Next**.
Select Web Service Extensions for Dynamic Content	ASP.NET
	Prohibit all Web service extensions not listed above
Select the Virtual Directories to Retain	None
Prevent Anonymous Users from Accessing Content Files	Deny anonymous users write access to content files.
IIS Settings Summary	Click **Next**.

Table 6-5. Security Configuration Wizard (continued)

14. At the **Save Security Policy** screen, click **Next**.

15. At the **Security Policy File Name** screen, type an appropriate name in the **Security policy file name** box and click **Next**.

16. In the dialog box that appears suggesting that a server restart is required, click **OK**.

17. At the **Apply Security Policy** screen, select **Apply Now** and click **Next**. An **Applying Security Policy** screen appears while the security policy is applied. This takes up to 2 minutes to complete.

18. At the **Applying Security Policy** screen, click **Next**.

19. At the **Completing the Security Configuration Wizard** screen, click **Finish**.

20. Restart the server for the security policies to take effect.

Enable Data Integrity Module

The Data Integrity Module enforces digital signing of all administrative data. For instructions on enabling this feature, consult the *Password Manager Administrator's Guide*.

If an administrator has created a Password Manager administrators group to allow multiple administrators to modify Password Manager components, additional configuration is required for the Data Integrity Module. The administrator must grant access to the Password Manager administrators group to authenticate to the service when the Data Integrity Module is enabled. To grant access for the Password Manager administrators to sign data settings, complete the following steps:

1. Launch Notepad.
2. Open the httpd.conf file found at C:\ProgramFiles\Common Files\Citrix\XTE\ conf.
3. Locate the XML section titled **<Files AuthenticatedWS.asmx>**.
4. Add another require group statement below the domain administrators statement specifying the domain name and the name of the Password Manager administrators group:

   ```
   require group "DOMAINNAME\\Password Manager
   Administrators"
   ```

5. Save and close the httpd.conf file.

CAUTION   The ServiceConfigurationTool.exe automatically replaces the httpd.conf file every time it is used to make changes to the service configuration. Manually complete the steps listed above after using the Service Configuration Tool to make changes in the Password Manager Service.

Configure Auditing

By default, most auditing is disabled in the Password Manager. To turn on the auditing feature, follow these steps:

1. Log on to the Password Manager Console.
2. Navigate to **Citrix Access Suite Console > Suite Components > Password Manager > User Configurations**.
3. Select the user configuration to edit from the menu.
4. Click **Edit User Configuration**.
5. Select **Client-side Interaction** from the menu on the left.
6. Click **Log Password Manager events using Windows event logging**.
7. Click **OK**.

Secure Password Manager Service Data

In exporting the service data, the Move Service Data Tool prompts administrators for a password to use as the basis for file encryption. Administrators should follow their organization's password policy when choosing a password to protect sensitive information. An example of this would be a 20-character password requiring both uppercase and nonalphabetic characters. The encrypted keys are exported to files for transfer to the other servers. A secure method of distribution would be to place the file on a removable medium such as a CD-ROM or a floppy disk and manually transfer the file to the other servers that are running the Password Manager Service. If administrators decide not to destroy the media containing the file after the transfer, they should store the media in a physically secure location in accordance with their security policy.

STEPS FOR SECURING CENTRAL STORE

The central store is divided into two areas: the synchronization area and the administrative data area. The synchronization area is a location that the Password Manager Agent contacts to obtain settings and store its encrypted secondary credentials. By default, the permissions on this location allow access only for the Password Manager administrators and the individual user. The administrative data area stores the administrative data used to create the agent settings for users. Administrative data include application definitions, password policies, and identity verification questions. By default, the administrative data area is secured to give only Password Manager administrators access.

The configuration and setup for both types of central store hosts are described below. The following steps for securing the central store will be discussed:

▼ Secure the operating system.

■ Secure the NTFS network share central store.

▲ Secure the Active Directory container central store.

Secure the Operating System

The Windows 2003 Security Configuration Wizard allows administrators to secure the operating system. It provides a mechanism to lock down the ports used by various services and disable Windows services that are unnecessary. The options that appear while the Windows Server 2003 Security Configuration Wizard is run vary with the choices made along the way.

To Install and Run Security Configuration Wizard

1. Log on to the server as a Windows user with local administrator rights.

2. Launch the Add or Remove Programs tool (**Start > Control Panel > Add or Remove Programs**).

3. Click **Add/Remove Windows Components** to bring up the **Windows Components Wizard.**

4. Select the **Security Configuration Wizard** check box and click **Next**. A number of progress messages temporarily appear.

5. When the installation is complete, click **Finish**.

6. Close the **Add or Remove Programs** dialog box.

7. Launch the Security Configuration Wizard **(Start > Administrative Tools > Security Configuration Wizard)**.

8. At the **Welcome** screen, click **Next**.

9. At the **Configuration Action** screen, ensure that **Create a new security policy** is selected and click **Next**.

10. At the **Select Server** screen, leave the default value and click **Next**.

11. At the **Processing Security Administrative Database** screen, wait for the system scan to complete and click **Next**.

12. At the **Role-Based Service Configuration** screen, click **Next**.

13. A **Select Server Roles** screen appears. The options that administrators should select from this screen vary with the machine to which they are applying the Security Configuration Wizard. These options are delineated for each component in Table 6-6.

NOTE   Administrators may have to modify these steps to account for installed software such as antivirus software and third-party firewalls.

14. At the **Save Security Policy** screen, click **Next**.

15. At the **Security Policy File Name** screen, type an appropriate name in the **Security policy file name** box and click **Next**.

16. In the dialog box that appears suggesting that a server restart is required, click **OK**.

17. At the **Apply Security Policy** screen, select **Apply Now** and click **Next**. An **Applying Security Policy** screen appears while the security policy is applied. This takes up to 2 minutes to complete.

18. At the **Applying Security Policy** screen, click **Next**.

19. At the **Completing the Security Configuration Wizard** screen, click **Finish**.

20. Restart the server for the security policies to take effect.

Screen	Options
Select Server Roles	Central Store using NTFS: File server
	Central Store using AD: N/A
Select Client Features	Automatic update client
	DHCP client (if server obtains address via DHCP)
	DNS client
	DNS registration client (if server obtains address via DHCP)
	Domain member
	Microsoft networking client
Select Administration and Other Options	Time synchronization
	Windows firewall
Select Additional Services	N/A
Handling Unspecified Services	Do not change the start-up mode of the service.
Confirm Service Changes	Click **Next**.
Network Security	Leave **Skip this section** cleared and click **Next**.
Open Ports and Approved Applications	445 (NTFS): Only on machines using an NTFS Network Share Central Store
	389 (LDAP): Only on machines using an AD Container Central Store
Confirm Port Configuration	Click **Next**.
Registry Settings	Leave **Skip this section** cleared and click **Next**.
Require SMB Security Signatures	Leave **All computers that connect to it satisfy the minimum operating system requirements** checked.
	Leave **It has surplus process capacity that can be used to sign the file and print traffic** checked.
	Click **Next**.
Outbound Authentication Methods	Domain accounts

(continued on next page)

Table 6-6. Security Configuration Wizard

Screen	Options
Outbound Authentication Using Domain Accounts	Windows NT 4.0 Service Pack 6a or later operating systems
Inbound Authentication Methods	N/A
Registry Settings Summary	Click **Next**.
Audit Policy	Leave the **Skip this section check box** cleared and click **Next**.
	Select **Audit successful and unsuccessful activities**.
	Click **Next**.
Internet Information Services	Select **Skip this section** and click **Next**.

Table 6-6.   Security Configuration Wizard (continued)

Secure NTFS Network Share Central Store

To permanently disable administrative shares on a server (Windows Server 2000/Windows Server 2003), follow these steps:

1. Launch regedit.exe.

2. Browse to **HKEY_LOCAL_MACHINE > SYSTEM > CurrentControlSet > Services > LanManServer > Parameters**.

3. Change the value of AutoShareServer to **0**.

   If AutoShareServer does not exist, create a registry key with this name of type REG_DWORD and set its value to **0**.

4. Restart the machine.

Once the administrative shares are disabled, the administrator can create and configure the central store. In a central store configured as an NTFS network share, up to three folders are used to store the different areas of the store. These folders are found in the root of the central store share.

The synchronization location is kept in a folder called People. This folder contains subfolders for each Password Manager user with appropriate permissions for reading and writing his or her credential data. The administrators have permissions to add and remove agent settings from users' folders. The administrative data are kept in a folder called CentralStoreRoot. By default, only administrators have permissions to **Read** and **Write** data within this folder. Finally, the domain hierarchy data is kept in a folder using the NetBIOS name for the domain. This folder is present only when one is using NT or Active Directory domains for primary authentication with the network share and contains the user configuration settings when they are assigned to organizational units or individual users. The folder contains subfolders that are named using the security identifier (SID) of the organizational unit (OU) or user to which the settings should be applied. By default, only administrators have read and write permissions to the domain folder, but users have **Read** permissions so that they can locate the settings that apply to them. Depending on the type of network share host, the types of permissions granted will be different.

By default, no permissions are allowed to propagate from the root share to the child folders: CentralStoreRoot and People. However, permissions assigned to the root folder are allowed to propagate to the domain folder. The File Synchronization Setup Utility automatically grants full control to the local administrators group for both the CentralStoreRoot and People folders and removes all permissions for authenticated users. No other folders are created by the utility.

The Password Manager Agent is responsible for creating subfolders inside the People folder and, upon their creation, sets the permissions of the folder to modify for the creator/owner and enables inheritable permissions to propagate from the parent folder. All remaining folders in the central store repository are created by the Password Manager Console during use as necessary. The console created the CentralStoreRoot\AdminConsole folder during discovery, and if an Active Directory domain is used, it creates a folder in the root of the central store share. During installation, the File Synchronization Setup Utility is run when the administrator uses the wizard to create an NTFS network share. To create and configure the central store, do the following:

1. Run the File Synchronization Setup Utility to create the root share and the two subfolders People and CentralStoreRoot. If the folders already have been created, go to the next step.

2. Grant the Password Manager Administrator account **Full Control** of the root share folder and both of the subfolders inside the shared folder.

3. Launch the console as a Password Manager administrator. This causes all subsequent folders and objects to be created with the appropriate Password Manager administrator permissions automatically.

4. Verify that the appropriate permissions are added to the **AdminConsole** folder.

Secure Active Directory Container Central Store

Securing a central store that is on the Active Directory requires the preparation of both the Active Directory schema and the domain. In environments with multiple administrators, permissions must be delegated to each new administrator.

Schema Preparation

The Active Directory Schema Extension Utility still must be run by a member of the schema administrators group for the target forest. This tool adds several classes and attributes to the forest schema, allowing the Password Manager to store user configuration and encrypted credential information as objects inside the Active Directory.

Domain Preparation

The Active Directory Domain Preparation Utility must be run by a member of the domain administrators group for the target domain.

When it is run without specifying a location, the utility affects the entire domain; however, if necessary, the tool can be run on a per-OU basis. To prepare an individual OU, provide the relative distinguished name of the OU on the command line after the executable name:

```
CTXDOMAINPREP CN=Users
```

NOTE The full distinguished name (CN=Users, DC=Example, DC=com) is not used because the tool automatically appends the distinguished name for the domain. If the administrator runs this command for more than one OU within the domain, he or she may receive a message indicating that a previous installation was found. This is normal behavior, as the tool expects to create the central store location each time it is executed.

Delegation Setup

With an Active Directory host for the central store, the synchronization and domain hierarchy data are stored in the individual containers for users and organizational units. The administrative data are stored in an application data partition under the domain root and can be viewed by using **ADSI Edit** (available from www.microsoft.com) by opening the appropriate domain and navigating down the following containers: **Program Data > Citrix > Metaframe Password Manager > CentralStoreRoot**.

All administrators accessing the central store will need appropriate permissions to the following containers:

▼ CN=CentralStoreRoot, CN=Metaframe Password Manager, CN=Citrix, CN= Program Data

■ Organizational unit containers to be managed

▲ User containers to be managed

The Active Directory Domain Preparation Utility assigns full control to the domain administrators group and SYSTEM account and restricts authenticated users to read and allows the SELF account to create and delete Citrix single sign-on (SSO) objects. For more information on the exact permissions assigned, see the *Password Manager Administrator's Guide*.

In an environment with multiple administrators, the recommended method of maintaining administrators is to create a Password Manager administrators group with permissions for the central store. After creating the group, assign the necessary permissions by following these steps:

1. Using **ADSI Edit**, navigate to the **Citrix > Program Data > Metaframe Password Manager > CentralStoreRoot** container.

2. Right click and choose **Properties** from the context menu.

3. Select the **Security** tab.

4. Click **Advanced...**

5. Click **Add** and enter the Password Manager Administrator group in the **Name** field.

6. Set the **Apply Onto** field to **This object and all Child Objects**.

7. Select the **Allow** checkbox for each of the following permissions:
   - List Contents
   - Read All Properties
   - Write All Properties
   - Delete
   - Delete Subtree
   - All Validated Writes
   - Create Container Objects
   - Delete Container Objects

8. Click **OK** to close the **Permission Entry** dialog.

9. Click **OK** to close the **Access Control Setting** dialog.

10. Click **OK** to close the **CentralStoreRoot properties** dialog.

11. Add all user accounts that need to administer the Password Manager to the **Password Manager Administrators** group.

Delegated Permissions

For each user account that will be a Password Manager administrator, the administrator must delegate control of the domain, OUs, or user accounts the Password Manager administrator will manage. If the user account will manage all user accounts or domain-level settings, it will need to have control delegated at the root of the domain. To delegate permissions for a user or group account, follow these steps:

1. Using **ADSI Edit**, navigate to the OU or domain object for the delegated permissions.

2. Right click on the OU or domain name (for domain-level permissions) and select **Properties**.

3. Select the **Security** tab.

4. Click **Advanced...**

5. Click **Add** and enter the Password Manager administrator's account in the **Name** field that will have administrator permissions for this OU or domain and then click **OK**.

6. Set the **Apply Onto** field to **This object and all Child Objects**.

7. Select the **Allow** checkbox for each of the following permissions:

   ■ Create citrix-SSOConfig Objects

   ■ Delete citrix-SSOConfig Objects

   ■ Create citrix-SSOLicense Class Objects

   ■ Delete citrix-SSOLicence Class Objects

8. Click **OK**.

9. Click **Add** and enter the Password Manager administrator's account in the **Name** field that will have administrator permissions for this OU or domain and then click **OK**.

10. Set the **Apply Onto** field to **User objects**.

11. Select the **Allow** checkbox for **Full Control**.

12. Click **OK**.

13. To grant Full Control for the Citrix objects, repeat steps 9 through 12, changing the **Apply Onto** field from **User objects** to each of the following object types:

   ■ Citrix-SSOConfig objects

   ■ Citrix-SSOLicenseClass objects

   ■ Citrix-SSOSecret objects

14. Click **OK** to close the **Access Control Setting** dialog.

15. Click **OK** to close the **OU Properties** dialog.

NOTE   The Active Directory Users & Computers MMC Snap-in does not provide access to all the Citrix class objects. The steps listed above have to be completed using ADSI Edit. Also, the Delegate Control Wizard may not properly assign the correct permissions, and so using ADSI Edit is recommended.

VERIFY SECURED CONFIGURATION

To verify that all the security steps have been followed, perform the following steps:

1. From a different machine, run a port scanner and verify that only the expected ports are open.

2. From a Password Manager Agent machine, verify that the agent icon is not in the system tray.

3. From a Password Manager Agent machine, open the Logon Manager and verify that no plaintext passwords can be displayed using the reveal option.

4. From a Password Manager Agent machine, go to a website that requires a logon and has not been configured for use with the Password Manager. Ensure that the users are not prompted to store credentials if they are not permitted to configure their own applications.

5. Attempt to log in to the Password Manager Console as a user who should not have access. This should result in an **access denied** error.

6. Using a third-party network monitor, start a network capture and record as an administrator logs into the Password Manager Console. Confirm that all traffic is encrypted.

7. From the NTFS Central Store machine, navigate to **Start > Run**. Enter the following text into the **Open** field:

   ```
   \\localhost\admin$
   ```

   Verify that the error message returned is "**No network provider accepted the given network path**."

SUMMARY

This chapter explained threats to the Citrix Password Manager, countermeasures to those threats, and ways to implement each countermeasure. Always keep the operating system, antivirus software, and Citrix Password Manager up to date with the latest security hot fixes and service packs.

CHAPTER 7

Presentation Server

This chapter explains how to protect the Citrix Presentation Server machine. The discussion covers the assets of the Presentation Server, threats to those assets, countermeasures to the threats, and instructions for implementing the countermeasures in a Presentation Server environment.

DEPLOYMENTS

Users remotely run published applications by using the Citrix Presentation Server Client. The client connects to a Presentation Server and launches a published application on that server. This connection is known as an ICA session. The client can establish an ICA session from the intranet via SSL Relay (Figure 7-1) or from the Internet via the Secure Gateway (Figure 7-2). Depending on an organization's network topology, the Presentation Server traffic may pass through multiple DMZs via the Secure Gateway and Secure Gateway Proxy (Figure 7-3). A group of Presentation Servers is known as a Presentation Server farm, or farm.

Session Reliability

Session reliability keeps ICA sessions active and on the user's screen when network connectivity is interrupted. Users continue to see the application they are using until network connectivity resumes.

The port that the Presentation Server Client will use to send ICA traffic over the network depends on whether session reliability is enabled and whether SSL Relay or Secure Gateway is in use. Table 7-1 indicates the default port to which the Presentation Server Client sends the ICA traffic.

COMPONENTS

The Presentation Server is composed of many services, subsystems, drivers, and executables; collectively, they are referred to here as components. The following material

	No SSL Relay, No Secure Gateway	SSL Relay	Secure Gateway Single-Hop	Secure Gateway Double-Hop
Session reliability disabled	1494	443	443	443
Session reliability enabled	2598	443	443	443

Table 7-1. ICA Traffic Ports

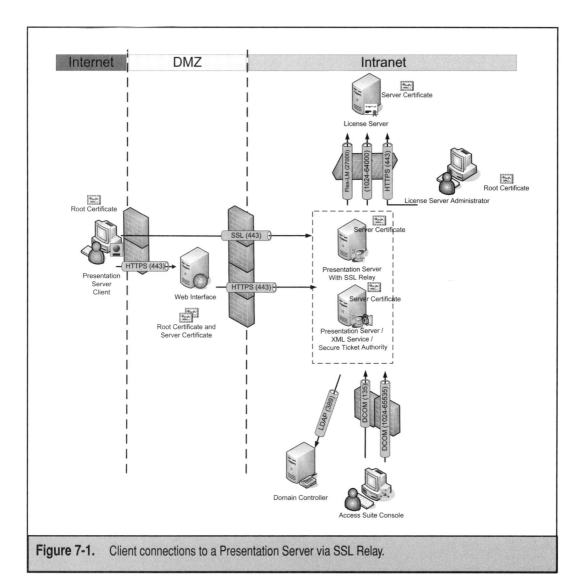

Figure 7-1.   Client connections to a Presentation Server via SSL Relay.

is not exhaustive; it is intended to give a brief overview of the major components of the Presentation Server. Not all components require configuration to be secured. These items may be listed in this section but will not be discussed further.

The primary components of the Presentation Server are as follows.

Access Suite Console

The Access Suite Console is the management interface to the Citrix Access Suite. The Access Suite Console is accessible only by Citrix administrators and provides a unified

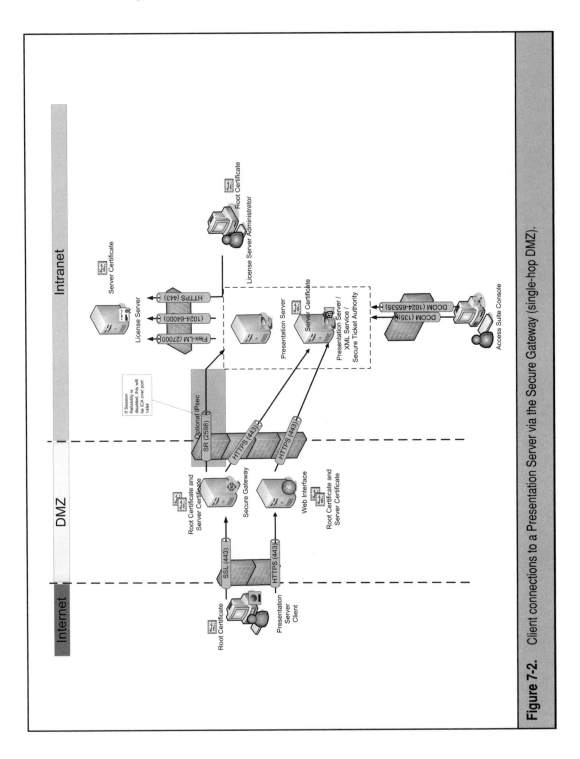

Figure 7-2.   Client connections to a Presentation Server via the Secure Gateway (single-hop DMZ).

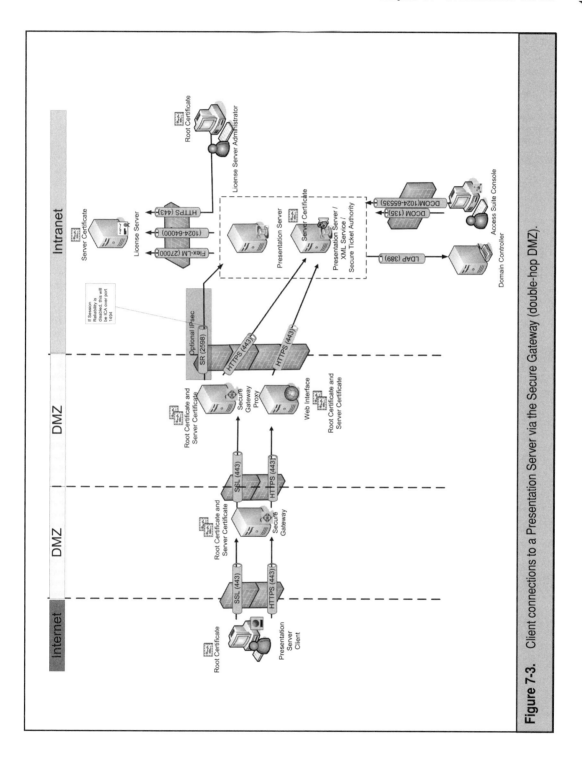

Figure 7-3.   Client connections to a Presentation Server via the Secure Gateway (double-hop DMZ).

means of administering different products in the Access Suite. The Access Suite Console is a different console from the Presentation Server Console. The Access Suite Console can be used to perform tasks such as the following:

▼ View alerts

■ View reports from the Report Center

■ Run the Diagnostic Facility

■ View applications published with the Presentation Server Console

■ Manage hot fixes

▲ Configure the Web Interface

Citrix Connection Configuration Utility

The Citrix Connection Configuration Utility adds support for more connection types and advanced configuration options than does the Terminal Services Configuration utility that ships with Windows Server 2003.

On Presentation Server 4.0 for 64-bit Windows Server 2003, the functionality of Citrix Connection Configuration is added to the Terminal Services Configuration utility by the Presentation Server.

Use the Citrix Connection Configuration utility to do the following:

▼ Add network, asynchronous, and other types of connections

■ Configure existing connections

■ Set parameters for mapping client devices

■ Set modem parameters

▲ Test modem configurations

Configuration Manager

The Configuration Manager service is used to fetch the configuration file for a centrally configured Web Interface. It is used only if the Web Interface is installed and configured to use a centralized configuration file.

CPU Utilization Management

CPU Utilization Management is a Presentation Server component that is used to enable CPU allotment policies between users and/or applications. CPU Utilization Management installs the Citrix CPU Utilization Mgmt/Resource Mgmt service, the Citrix CPU Utilization Mgmt/User-Session Sync service, and the Citrix CPU Utilization Management/User-Session Synchronization service. These services are disabled by default.

Client Network

The Client Network service is used to map Presentation Server Client drives and devices to the ICA session.

Diagnostic Facility COM Server

The Diagnostic Facility COM Server is used to troubleshoot incompatibilities and errors that can occur when third-party applications are running in a Presentation Server environment.

Encryption Service

The encryption service is used to generate random data that are needed during Secure ICA session handshakes.

Independent Management Architecture Service

The Independent Management Architecture (IMA) service allows application publishing settings and policies to be shared among a farm of Presentation Servers. IMA is responsible for ensuring that configuration changes remain consistent across the farm and is used to communicate the availability of individual servers.

All IMA data are stored in a database known as the IMA data store. The IMA data store is a database where IMA stores all Presentation Server configuration and policy settings. IMA supports several Structured Query Language (SQL) database back ends.

For performance, each Presentation Server stores a subset of the IMA data store in a cache known as the Local Host Cache. This cache is stored locally on each Presentation Server machine and is maintained by IMA. The cache maintains a subset of information that is stored in the IMA data store.

Installation Manager

The Installation Manager provides an automated way to deploy new applications, upgrades, service packs, and files to the Presentation Servers in a farm. The Installation Manager relies on the ADF Installer service to perform application installations.

Citrix WMI Service

The WMI service is used to give the Presentation Server's provider for Microsoft Windows Management Instrumentation (WMI) access to IMA events.

Load Manager

The Load Manager is used to balance published application loads across a Presentation Server farm. The Load Manager also can be used to tune server loads on specific Presentation Servers to help ensure an optimal load across a Presentation Server farm.

Memory Optimization

Memory optimization is used to rebase server applications to improve memory usage. This feature installs and uses the Citrix Virtual Memory Optimization service. This service is disabled by default.

MFCOM

The MFCOM service provides a programmatic way to configure the Presentation Server and the associated components. The configuration options available through the Access Suite Console are available through the MFCOM interface. MFCOM allows Citrix administrators to automate common tasks that would have to be performed by the Presentation Server Console and Access Suite Console by allowing scripts to be written in VB or .NET to communicate with a Presentation Server through the MFCOM interface.

Network Manager

The Network Manager provides third-party management by allowing configuration options and settings to be viewed by using Simple Network Management Protocol (SNMP). The Network Manager provides an SNMP agent that is loaded by the Microsoft Windows SNMP service. SNMP traps can be monitored by using third-party SNMP consoles such as Tivoli NetView, HP OpenView, and CA Unicenter.

Pass-Through Client

The Pass-Through Client is a form of the Presentation Server Client that allows it to be used as a published application. Its behavior is slightly different from that of the Presentation Server Client that is run from workstations and laptops. Presentation Server users launch the Pass-Through Client as a published application. The Pass-Through Client in turn connects to a second Presentation Server and runs either another published application or a desktop. The Pass-Through Client therefore relays the ICA session from the second Presentation Server to the client on the user's client machine.

Presentation Server Console

The Presentation Server Console is used to configure the Presentation Server. Using the Presentation Server Console, Citrix administrators can publish applications and modify policies that control client devices and session behavior.

Use the Presentation Server Console to manage any server farm in a deployment. Use the Presentation Server Console to do the following:

▼ Configure server and farm settings

■ Create administrator accounts and delegate tasks

■ Create policies for users' connections

- View information about current sessions, users, and processes
- Set up and manage printers for users
- Publish applications and monitor application usage
- Monitor, reset, disconnect, and reconnect sessions
- Send messages to users and shadow their sessions
- Deploy Installation Manager packages
- ▲ Configure the Load Manager

Presentation Server Management Pack for Microsoft Operations Manager

The Management Pack is a plug-in to the Microsoft Operations Manager that enables system administrators to monitor the health and availability of Presentation Server Enterprise Edition servers and server farms and anticipate and react quickly to the many problems that may occur.

The Management Pack interprets and reports on information supplied by

- ▼ The Presentation Server Provider that runs on Enterprise Edition servers
- The Licensing Provider that runs on license servers
- ▲ System events generated on Enterprise Edition servers

Print Manager Service

The Print Manager service is used to map printers to the ICA session.

Resource Manager

The Resource Manager consists of the Resource Manager service, the Resource Manager Mail service, and the summary database.

The Resource Manager service manages resources on a Presentation Server or a farm of Presentation Servers. The Resource Manager can be configured to collect and store data related to system performance, user activity, processor usage, and application usage. The Resource Manager can report on application availability, server availability, server performance, and application usage.

The Resource Manager (RM) Mail service works in conjunction with the RM service. The purpose of the RM Mail service is to send e-mail when a predetermined system state is reached. For example, an RM threshold setting could be configured to generate an event, causing an e-mail to a Citrix administrator to be sent when the number of concurrent users on a Presentation Server reaches 100.

The Resource Manager Summary database is used to store Resource Manager–related events on a Presentation Server. The Resource Manager Summary database is the central collection point of this information on a Presentation Server.

Secure Ticket Authority

The Secure Ticket Authority is a component of the XML service that exchanges Presentation Server information for randomly generated tickets. It is used to control access for the Secure Gateway.

Web Interface servers request tickets at application launch time by sending Presentation Server information to the STA as part of a ticket request. The data sent to the STA include the address of the Presentation Server to which the user will connect and extended information about the name of the current user and the published application the user intends to launch. The STA responds by generating a ticket and sending it back to the Web Interface. This ticket and its corresponding data remain in memory at the STA for a configurable number of seconds.

SSL Relay

The Citrix SSL Relay provides encryption, authentication, and forwarding capabilities for ICA connections and other traffic. This component is hosted in the XTE Server. It must be configured on all Presentation Servers to which clients will attempt SSL/TLS connections. Typically, the Citrix SSL Relay listens for SSL/TLS traffic on TCP port 443 and decrypts and forwards information to other services on the server, such as the XML service.

Suite Monitoring and Alerting Service

The Suite Monitoring and Alerting service watches the event log and Windows Management Instrumentation Provider for the Presentation Server for problems and raises alerts in the Access Management Console. This service is disabled by default.

Windows Management Instrumentation Provider

The Windows Management Instrumentation Provider for the Presentation Server supplies information about servers and server farms. This information is displayed by the Presentation Server Management Pack, which is a plug-in to Microsoft Operations Manager.

XML Service

The Citrix XML service provides published application information to Presentation Server clients and Web Interface servers. This service functions as the contact point between the Presentation Server farm and the Web Interface servers. The XML service can be hosted by IIS or the XTE Server.

XTE Server

The Citrix XTE Server is a service endpoint or proxy for TCP/IP protocols used by the Presentation Server. The XTE Server hosts the session reliability component and the SSL

Relay component for forwarding network traffic inside an SSL/TLS tunnel within CPS. It also can host the XML service.

ACCOUNTS

The Presentation Server installs multiple custom user accounts to support parts of the functionality of the Presentation Server that must operate as a particular user account or with specific Windows privileges.

Anonymous Accounts

During the installation of the Presentation Server, a special local Windows user group called Anonymous is created. This group is created with 15 local users named Anon001 through Anon015. The AnonXXX users have guest permissions by default. These accounts differ from other user groups in that they have a default 10-minute idle time before they are logged out. All user information, desktop settings, and user-specific files are removed when the account is logged out or the ICA session is terminated.

Service Accounts

The Presentation Server installs two accounts for services that need to run with one or more specific privileges or permissions.

Ctx_SmaUser

The Ctx_SmaUser account is used to run the Suite Monitoring and Alerting service and the Print Manager service.

Ctx_ConfigMgr

The Ctx_ConfigMgr account is used to run the Configuration Manager for the Web Interface.

CITRIX ADMINISTRATOR

A user account can be designated as a Citrix administrator. The Citrix administrator role means that the user has been assigned special administrative privileges for managing Citrix components. Citrix administrator tasks may include configuring published applications, setting up device and connection policies, and monitoring usage information. Citrix administrators are not synonymous with Windows administrators. Citrix administrators' roles are controlled via object-based delegated administration permissions. The Citrix administrator role can be assigned during Presentation Server installation or by using the Presentation Server console.

ASSETS

A Presentation Server environment has three categories of assets:

▼ Presentation Server assets, which are parts of the Presentation Server software

■ Presentation Server machine assets, which make up the environment in which the Presentation Server runs, including the underlying hardware, operating system, and applications

▲ ICA session assets, which belong to the session that the Presentation Server hosts for a particular user that is running a published application

Presentation Server

The assets of Presentation Server are as follows:

▼ *Access Suite Console.* The security characteristics of this asset are integrity and availability.

■ *Anonymous accounts.* The security characteristics of this asset are confidentiality, integrity, and availability.

■ *Citrix administrator accounts.* The security characteristics of this asset are confidentiality, integrity, and availability.

■ *Configuration data settings.* The security characteristics of this asset are confidentiality, integrity, and availability.

■ *Desktop session.* The security characteristics of this asset are availability, confidentiality, and integrity.

■ *Device mapping.* The security characteristics of this asset are availability, confidentiality, and integrity.

■ *IMA data store.* The security characteristics of this asset are availability, confidentiality, and integrity.

■ *IMA service.* The security characteristics of this asset are availability, confidentiality, and integrity.

■ *Installation Manager.* The security characteristics of this asset are confidentiality, integrity, and availability.

■ *License Server session data.* The security characteristics of this asset are confidentiality, integrity, and availability.

■ *Load Manager.* The security characteristics of this asset are availability and integrity.

■ *Local Host Cache.* The security characteristics of this asset are availability, confidentiality, and integrity.

■ *MFCOM service.* The security characteristic of this asset is availability.

■ *Network Manager.* The security characteristics of this asset are availability, confidentiality, and integrity.

■ *Pass-Through Client.* The security characteristic of this asset is availability.

■ *Presentation Server Console.* The security characteristics of this asset are availability, confidentiality, and integrity.

■ *Resource Manager Mail service.* The security characteristics of this asset are availability, confidentiality, and integrity.

■ *Resource Manager service.* The security characteristics of this asset are availability, confidentiality, and integrity.

■ *Resource Manager summary database.* The security characteristics of this asset are availability, confidentiality, and integrity.

■ *Secure Gateway session data.* The security characteristics of this asset are confidentiality and integrity.

■ *Secure Ticket Authority.* The security characteristics of this asset are availability, confidentiality, and integrity.

■ *Suite Monitoring and Alerting service.* The security characteristics of this asset are availability, confidentiality, and integrity.

■ *SSL Relay.* The security characteristics of this asset are availability, confidentiality, and integrity.

■ *Web Interface session data.* The security characteristics of this asset are confidentiality and integrity.

■ *XML service.* The security characteristics of this asset are availability, confidentiality, and integrity.

▲ *XTE Server.* The security characteristics of this asset are availability, confidentiality, and integrity.

Presentation Server Machine

The assets of the Presentation Server machine are as follows:

▼ *Access to the intranet.* The security characteristics of this asset are confidentiality and availability.

■ *Application files.* The security characteristics of this asset are integrity and availability.

■ *Clipboard data.* The security characteristics of this asset are confidentiality and integrity.

■ *COM ports.* The security characteristics of this asset are confidentiality and integrity.

■ *LPT ports.* The security characteristics of this asset are confidentiality and integrity.

- *Server operating system.* The security characteristics of this asset are integrity and availability.
- *Smart card reader.* The security characteristics of this asset are confidentiality and availability.
- ▲ *System files.* The security characteristics of this asset are integrity and availability.

ICA Session

The assets of an ICA session on the Presentation Server are as follows:

- ▼ *ICA browsing session data between the Presentation Server Client and the Presentation Server.* The security characteristics of this asset are confidentiality and integrity.
- *ICA session client.* The security characteristics of this asset are confidentiality, integrity, and availability.
- *ICA session data between the Presentation Server Client and the Presentation Server.* The security characteristics of this asset are confidentiality and integrity.
- *ICA session data between the Secure Gateway and the Presentation Server.* The security characteristics of this asset are confidentiality, integrity, and availability.
- *ICA session files.* The security characteristics of this asset are confidentiality and integrity.
- *User password.* The security characteristics of this asset are confidentiality and integrity.
- ▲ *User smart card PIN.* The security characteristics of this asset are confidentiality and integrity.

THREATS AND COUNTERMEASURES

There are threats and countermeasures for the Presentation Server, Presentation Server Machine, and ICA session assets.

Presentation Server

The threats to the Presentation Server include

- ▼ Unauthorized access to configuration settings (including the IMA data store)
- Unauthorized access to the Presentation Server Console and Access Suite Console
- Unauthorized access to SNMP data
- Unauthorized access to Secure Ticket Authority login tickets
- Unauthorized access to Installation Manager packages
- ▲ Unauthorized access to Resource Manager Mail service e-mails

Unauthorized Access to Configuration Settings (Including IMA Data Store)

Presentation Server configuration settings are stored inside the registry, the IMA, and in some cases the configuration files. Tampering with these settings can cause the server to become unresponsive, enabling a denial of service; behave in an unintended fashion; or have critical pieces of functionality disabled. Modification of some settings, such as the published application settings, may lead to policy violations that allow malicious users to execute unintended applications on the Presentation Server. The configuration settings and components at risk include

▼ Configuration data

■ Published application settings

■ Printer settings

■ ICA encryption settings

■ Presentation Server policies

▲ Citrix administrator role assignments

Countermeasures Configuration data stored in registry keys and configuration files stored on the file system are protected against unauthorized modifications by ACLs that are configured during the installation of the Presentation Server. Settings stored within IMA are accessible only by authenticated Citrix administrators. The connection to the SQL database back end that hosts the IMA data store must be secured and be accessible only by authorized database administrators.

Unauthorized Access to Presentation Server Console and Access Suite Console

The administrative consoles that enable remote configuration of the Presentation Server are the Presentation Server Console and the Access Suite Console.

Countermeasures The Presentation Server Console and Access Suite Console both communicate with a Presentation Server over the network. The Access Suite Console authenticates the administrator by using COM impersonation. To limit the exposure to network-level attacks to the administrative consoles in a Presentation Server environment, do the following:

▼ Segment the Presentation Server farm on its own network segment. TCP ports 2513 and 135 for the Presentation Server Console and the Access Suite Console should not be accessible from outside the farm. Instead, the consoles should be available as published applications to authorized Citrix administrators.

■ Secure administrative console connections by using IPsec or an SSL VPN.

■ Access the Presentation Server Console only as a published application.

▲ Access the Access Suite Console only as a published application.

Unauthorized Access to SNMP Data

Unauthorized access to SNMP data will lead to information disclosure. It may enable an attacker to access information about the running state of a Presentation Server. If configured incorrectly, it may enable an attacker to update SNMP settings.

Countermeasures Countermeasures to these threats include the following:

▼ Install and enable Presentation Server SNMP only if it is needed.

■ Disable the Windows SNMP service if it is not needed.

■ Change the default SNMP community string. Do not make the string a predictable value.

■ Restrict access to SNMP. Create a white list of servers that are allowed to send SNMP queries to the server.

■ Limit the allowed SNMP messages to "get" messages only. Deny all set messages.

▲ Consider securing SNMP with IPsec.

Unauthorized Access to STA Login Tickets

Unauthorized access to STA login tickets may enable an attacker to compromise ICA sessions and impersonate clients to gain unauthorized access to the Presentation Server.

Countermeasures Countermeasures to these threats include the following:

▼ Configure SSL Relay to secure STA communication.

▲ Configure IPsec to secure STA communication.

Unauthorized Access to Installation Manager Packages

Unauthorized access to Installation Manager packages may enable an attacker to replace packages that are to be installed on the Presentation Server. This will allow the attacker to install custom software on the Presentation Server.

Countermeasures Countermeasures to these threats include the following:

▼ Disable the Installation Manager if it is not needed.

■ Use strong ACLs on the Installation Manager Package network share.

■ Do not grant Installation Manager delegated permissions to Citrix administrators who do not need them.

▲ Configure auditing.

Unauthorized Access to Resource Manager Mail Service E-Mails

Unauthorized access to Resource Manager Mail service e-mails is a form of information disclosure. Access to this information will enable an attacker to learn statistics about the

Presentation Server and clients. This information may be used to gain further access into the enterprise through the use of other malicious methods.

Countermeasures   Countermeasures to these threats include the following:

▼ Disable the use of Resource Manager Mail service if it is not needed.

▲ Use IPsec to secure communication with the Microsoft Exchange Server.

Presentation Server Machine

The threats to the Presentation Server machine include

▼ Unauthorized logon to the Presentation Server machine

■ Unauthorized access to server devices

■ Unauthorized access to server system files

▲ Service disruption

Unauthorized Logon to Presentation Server Machine

Unauthorized logon to the Presentation Server occurs when a user executes Presentation Server functionality in violation of organizational policy. Attackers can gain unauthorized logon to the Presentation Server either remotely or physically.

If an attacker physically logs in to the Presentation Server, several attacks are possible, such as the following:

▼ Restarting the machine and using various tools to circumvent operating system security

▲ Logging in at the console

If someone can remotely send traffic to the Presentation Server, that person can launch network-based attacks against the operating system and services running on the server. The goal of these remote attacks may be to log in remotely to the Presentation Server host.

Countermeasures   Countermeasures to unauthorized access to Presentation Server include

▼ Restricting who can physically reach the Presentation Server

■ Restricting the number of Windows accounts on the Presentation Server host

■ Setting appropriate ACLs on configuration and log files

■ Restricting logon to the console

■ Removing Remote Desktop Protocol access

▲ Disabling server functionality that is not needed

Unauthorized Access to Server Devices

Devices that are connected to the server computer may be vulnerable to tampering or information disclosure attacks if a malicious user connects to the server. If the devices do not need to be accessed in an ICA session, ICA session access to them can be disabled. These server devices include

▼ Printers

■ Serial and parallel ports

■ CD-ROM drives

▲ Floppy disk drives

Countermeasures Countermeasures to this threat include the following:

▼ Disable ICA session access to server devices that do not need to be accessed by users.

■ Configure group policy to restrict access to CD-ROM drives attached to the Presentation Server machine.

▲ Configure group policy to restrict access to floppy drives attached to the Presentation Server machine.

Unauthorized Access to Server System Files

System files stored on the server machine, such as files that belong to the operating system and installed applications, may be vulnerable to disclosure or tampering. Unauthorized users may deliberately modify files in an attempt to gain control of the Presentation Server machine. Authorized users may accidentally modify or delete system files.

Countermeasures Countermeasures to this threat in the Presentation Server include the following:

▼ Allow read-only access to system files only for users.

■ Run published applications only as a nonprivileged user.

■ Disable client drive mapping if it is not needed.

■ Disable clipboard mapping if it is not needed.

▲ Disable administrative shares.

Service Disruption

Service disruptions must be planned for. They can be caused by nonmalicious or malicious activity. Service disruptions can be caused by

▼ *System failure*

■ Software failures

■ Hardware failures

■ Power failures

■ *Human error*

  ■ Accidental deletion of files

  ■ Misconfiguration

▲ *Malicious behavior*

  ■ Denial-of-service attacks

Countermeasures Countermeasures to nonmalicious disruptions of service include

▼ Restricting access to Presentation Server administration functions

▲ Using backups

Countermeasures to denial-of-service attacks include audit trails.

ICA Session

The threats to the ICA session on the Presentation Server are

▼ Disclosure of credentials

■ Disclosure of ICA session data

■ Disclosure of user files

▲ Tampering with user files

Disclosure of Credentials

The password or smart card PIN employed by the user to authenticate to a Presentation Server must be protected when it is sent across the network to a server. This secret information may be disclosed to a third party that has access to the network if the ICA session data is not encrypted.

Countermeasures The countermeasures to the threat of password disclosure while it is in transit to the Presentation Server include the following:

▼ Use Kerberos authentication. The password or PIN will not be sent across the network.

■ Use strong authentication such as a one-time password token to mitigate the risk of credential disclosure.

▲ Use SSL/TLS to protect the confidentiality of the credentials.

Disclosure of ICA Session Data

The data transmitted during an ICA session may contain screen display or keystrokes that describe confidential information. This network traffic may be observed by an attacker if it is sent across a network unencrypted.

Countermeasures   The countermeasures to this threat are as follows:

▼   Protect the confidentiality of data communicated between the Presentation Server and Presentation Server Clients with SSL/TLS.

■   Configure the Presentation Server Clients to not store screen updates in the client bitmap disk cache. For more information, see Chapter 8, "Presentation Server Client."

■   Do not allow clients to establish ICA sessions that are not encrypted. This can be achieved by not permitting access to port 1494 from the network so that ICA connections must route through SSL Relay.

▲   Disable clipboard mapping on the server if it is not needed.

Disclosure of User Files

Files belonging to individual users that are stored on the Presentation Server machine may be vulnerable to disclosure when at rest on the server machine as well as in transit, when they are sent across the network to a client.

Countermeasures   The countermeasures to this threat in the Presentation Server include the following:

▼   Do not store user files on the Presentation Server machine.

■   Use SSL/TLS for all network communication to protect the confidentiality of the files.

■   Disable client drive mapping if it is not needed.

■   Disable clipboard mapping if it is not needed.

▲   Restrict users' access to files on the server machine.

Tampering with User Files

Files belonging to individual users that are stored on the server machine may be vulnerable to tampering via the ICA session when at rest on the server machine as well as in transit if they are sent across the network to a Presentation Server Client. All files on the server machine may be at risk if the ICA session is run by an administrator.

Countermeasures   The countermeasures to this threat in the Presentation Server include the following:

▼   Do not store user files on the Presentation Server machine.

■   Use SSL/TLS to protect the integrity of all network communication.

■   Disable client drive mapping if it is not needed.

■   Disable clipboard mapping if it is not needed.

▲   Run published applications only as a nonprivileged user.

STEPS FOR SECURING THE PRESENTATION SERVER

The following steps to secure the Presentation Server are discussed below:

▼ Secure the operating system.

■ Configure authentication.

■ Configure secure communications.

■ Configure client drive mapping.

■ Configure clipboard mapping.

■ Configure client device mapping.

■ Secure the IMA data store.

■ Configure Citrix administrator accounts.

■ Configure Citrix Connection Configuration.

■ Configure Terminal Services Configuration.

■ Configure Presentation Server policies.

■ Configure Group Policy for the Presentation Server.

■ Secure the SNMP configuration.

■ Secure IMA communication.

■ Access the Presentation Server Console only as a published application.

■ Access the Access Suite Console only as a published application.

■ Secure printer connections.

■ Secure Installation Manager deployments.

■ Secure the XML Service and Secure Ticket Authority.

■ Launch only published applications.

■ Secure the Pass-Through Client.

■ Run published applications only as a nonprivileged user.

■ Remove Remote Desktop Protocol access.

■ Disable administrative shares.

▲ Configure auditing.

Secure the Operating System

The Windows 2003 Security Configuration Wizard allows administrators to secure the operating system. It provides a mechanism to lock down the ports used by various services and disable Windows services that are unnecessary. The options that appear while one is running the Windows Server 2003 Security Configuration Wizard vary with the choices made along the way.

The applications listed in the "Open Ports and Approved Applications" section will differ depending on the role of the Presentation Server and which Presentation Server features are required. For example, not all Presentation Servers must communicate with Web Interface or run the Secure Ticket Authority.

NOTE Administrators may have to modify these steps to account for installed software such as antivirus or firewall software.

To install and run the Security Configuration Wizard, do the following:

1. Log on to the server as a Windows administrator.
2. Launch the Add or Remove Programs tool (**Start > Control Panel > Add or Remove Programs**).
3. Click **Add/Remove Windows Components** to bring up the **Windows Components Wizard.**
4. Select the **Security Configuration Wizard** check box and click **Next**. A number of progress messages temporarily appear.
5. When the installation is complete, click **Finish**.
6. Close the **Add or Remove Programs** dialog box.
7. Launch the Security Configuration Wizard (**Start > Administrative Tools > Security Configuration Wizard**).
8. At the **Welcome** screen, click **Next**.
9. At the **Configuration Action** screen, ensure that **Create a new security policy** is selected and click **Next**.
10. At the **Select Server** screen, leave the default value and click **Next**.
11. At the **Processing Security Configuration Database** screen, wait for the system scan to complete and click **Next**.
12. At the **Role-Based Service Configuration** screen, click **Next**.
13. The options that administrators should select from the **Select Server Roles** screen vary with the machine to which they are applying the Security Configuration wizard. Each of the subsequent screens requires selection of the different options shown in Table 7-2.
14. At the **Save Security Policy** screen, click **Next**.
15. At the **Security Policy File Name** screen, type an appropriate name in the **Security policy file name** box and click **Next**.
16. In the dialog box that appears suggesting that a server restart is required, click **OK**.

Screen	Options
Select Server Roles	Terminal server
Select Client Features	Automatic update client
	DHCP Client*
	*Required only if the server needs DHCP
	DNS client
	DNS registration client
	Domain member
	Microsoft networking client
Select Administration and Other Options	Time synchronization
	Windows firewall
	IPsec services
	Local Application installation
Select Additional Services	ADF Installer Service
	Citrix CPU Utilization Mgmt/Resource Mgmt
	Citrix CPU Utilization Mgmt/User-Session Sync
	Citrix Print Manager Service
	Citrix SMA Service
	Citrix Virtual Memory Optimization
	Citrix WMI Service
	Citrix XML Service
	Citrix XTE Server
	Client network
	Diagnostic Facility COM Server
	Encryption Service
	Independent Management Architecture
	MetaFrame COM Server
	Resource Manager Mail
Handling Unspecified Services	Do not change the start-up mode of the service.
Confirm Service Changes	Click **Next**.

(continued on next page)

Table 7-2.   Security Configuration Wizard

Screen	Options
Network Security	Leave **Skip this section** cleared and click **Next**.
Open Ports and Approved Applications	123 (NTP) (note that this is needed only if an external time server is used)
	1494 (note that if all ICA connections should use SSL Relay, do not add this port so that all ICA connections will be forced to connect through SSL Relay)
	Ports used by ADF Installer Service (AgentSVC.exe)
	Ports used by Diagnostic Facility COM Server (CDFSvc.exe)
	Ports used by Client Network (cdmsvc.exe)
	Ports used by Citrix Print Manager Service (CpSvc.exe)
	Ports used by Encryption Service (encsvc.exe)
	Ports used by Independent Management Architecture (ImaSrv.exe)
	Ports used by Resource Manager Mail (MailService.exe)
	Ports used by MetaFrame COM Server (mfcom.exe)
	Ports used by Citrix SMA Service (SmaService.exe)
	Ports used by System RPC applications
	Ports used by Citrix XTE Server (XTE.exe)
	Ports used by Citrix WMI Service (ctxwmisvc.exe)
	Ports used by Citrix XML Service (ctxxmlss.exe)
Confirm Port Configuration	Click **Next**.
Registry Settings	Leave **Skip this section** cleared and click **Next**.
Require SMB Security Signatures	Leave **All computers that connect to it satisfy the minimum operating system requirements** checked.

Table 7-2.   Security Configuration Wizard (continued)

Screen	Options
	Leave **It has surplus process capacity that can be used to sign the file and print traffic** checked.
	Click **Next**.
Outbound Authentication Methods	Domain accounts
Outbound Authentication Using Domain Accounts	Windows NT 4.0 Service Pack 6a or later operating systems
Inbound Authentication Methods	N/A
Registry Settings Summary	Click **Next**.
Audit Policy	Check the **Skip this section** box and click **Next**.
Audit Policy Summary	Click **Next**.

Table 7-2.   Security Configuration Wizard (continued)

17. At the **Apply Security Policy** screen, select **Apply Now** and click **Next**. An **Applying Security Policy** screen appears while the security policy is applied. This takes up to 2 minutes to complete.

18. At the **Applying Security Policy** screen, click **Next**.

19. At the **Completing the Security Configuration Wizard** screen, click **Finish**.

20. Restart the server for the security policies to take effect.

NOTE   After completing these steps, administrators will still have to follow their regular procedures for securing a server.

Configure Authentication

The Presentation Server supports enhanced forms of authentication that protect users' credentials as well as the Presentation Server from attacks on identity. The supported methods are

▼   Kerberos

■   Smart cards

▲   Passwords

NOTE For a detailed discussion of authentication methods supported in Citrix environments, refer to Chapter 2, "Secure Deployments."

Configure Kerberos Authentication

The Presentation Server Client for Windows features enhanced security for pass-through authentication. Rather than sending user passwords over the network, pass-through authentication leverages Kerberos authentication in combination with Security Support Provider Interface (SSPI) security exchange mechanisms. Kerberos is an industry-standard network authentication protocol that is built into the Windows operating systems.

System Requirements Kerberos logon requires Presentation Server 3.0 or 4.0 and Presentation Server Clients for Windows Version 9.x or later and works only between clients and servers that belong to the same or to trusted Windows 2000 or Windows 2003 domains. Servers must also be **trusted for delegation**, an option that is configured in the **Active Directory Users and Computers** management tool.

Kerberos logon is not available in the following circumstances:

▼ Connections for which any of the following options are selected in **Terminal Services Configuration**:

■ On the **General** tab, the **Use standard Windows authentication** option.

■ On the **Logon Settings** tab, the **Always use the following logon information** option or the **Always prompt for password** option.

■ Connections routed through the Secure Gateway.

■ If the server running the Presentation Server requires smart card logon.

▲ If the authenticated user account requires a smart card for interactive logon.

Kerberos support in the Presentation Server requires **XML Service DNS address resolution** to be enabled for the server farm or **reverse DNS resolution** to be enabled for the active directory domain.

To Enable Trust for Delegation All the Presentation Server computers in the farm must be trusted for delegation; this is configured on the domain controller.

1. Click **Start > Administrative Tools > Active Directory Users and Computers.**

2. Right click on the Presentation Server computer.

3. Click **Properties.**

4. Click on the **General** tab.

5. Check the **Trust computer for delegation** check box.

6. Click **OK.**

7. Repeat steps 2 through 6 for all Presentation Servers in the farm.

To Enable XML Service DNS Address Resolution

1. In the Presentation Server Console, select the farm to enable DNS address resolution.

2. From the **Actions** menu, select **Properties**. The farm **Properties** page appears.

3. Select **Settings**.

4. Check **Enable XML Service DNS address resolution**.

5. Click **OK**.

Terminal Services Configuration   There are some Terminal Services configuration options that prevent Kerberos from working. Because of this, they must be configured before Kerberos is used for authentication.

1. Click **Start > Administrative Tools > Terminal Services Configuration**.

2. In the left pane of the **Terminal Services Configuration** window, click on the **Connections** node.

3. In the right pane of the **Terminal Services Configuration** window, right click on the **ICA-tcp** connection.

4. Click **Properties**.

5. In the **ICA-tcp Properties** window, click the **General** tab.

6. Ensure that the **Use standard Windows authentication** check box is not checked.

7. Click the **Logon Settings** tab.

8. Ensure that the **Always prompt for password** check box is not checked.

Presentation Server Client Configuration   The client also needs configuration for Kerberos. For more information, see the section on Kerberos in Chapter 8, "Presentation Server Client."

Configure Smart Card Authentication

Users can authenticate to Presentation Server with smart cards. For a detailed discussion of smart cards, see Chapter 2, "Secure Deployments."

Smart Card Software Requirements   This section presents the basic guidelines for using smart cards with the Presentation Server. Consult the organization's smart card vendor or integrator to determine detailed configuration requirements for a particular vendor's smart card implementation.

The following components are required on the server:

▼   PC/SC software

▲   Cryptographic Service Provider (CSP) software

These components are required on the device that is running the supported Presentation Server Client:

▼ PC/SC software

■ Smart card reader software drivers

▲ Smart card reader

The Windows server and client operating systems may come with PC/SC, CSP, or smart card reader drivers already present. Consult the smart card vendor for information about whether these software components are supported or must be replaced with vendor-specific software.

Smart Card Configuration A complete and secure smart card solution can be relatively complicated, and Citrix recommends consulting the smart card vendor or integrator for details. Configuration of smart card implementations and configuration of third-party security systems such as certificate authorities are beyond the scope of this book.

Windows Policies for Smart Cards Microsoft Windows supports two security policy settings for interactive logon to a server session. Presentation Server Client sessions can utilize the following policies:

▼ *Require a smart card for interactive session logon.* This is a user policy that requires the user to insert a smart card for authentication.

▲ *Smart-card removal policy.* This is a computer policy that determines the behavior when the user removes the smart card from the smart card reader.

Configure Password Authentication

If neither Kerberos nor smart card authentication can be enabled, passwords can be used for authentication. Refer to the section on ICA session threats and countermeasures for the countermeasures that are needed to protect the password.

Configure Secure Communications

Traffic between Presentation Servers and the following components must be secured:

▼ Presentation Server Clients

▲ Web Interface servers

In some deployments, it is possible to use Microsoft Internet Information Services to secure the communication path between the Presentation Server and the Web Interface server. In other deployments, it is possible to use SSL Relay to secure the communication path between the Web Interface server and the Presentation Server. SSL Relay and SecureICA both can be used to secure the connection between the Presentation Server Client and the Presentation Server. For deployments that use the Secure Gateway, see Chapter 4, "Secure Gateway."

Citrix SSL Relay

Citrix SSL Relay provides end-to-end SSL/TLS encryption between specific servers and clients. SSL Relay is useful when

▼ The Presentation Server farm is small.

▲ End-to-end encryption of data between clients and servers is required.

SSL Relay operates as an intermediary in the communications between the client and the Citrix XML Service and/or the ICA listener running on each server. Each client authenticates SSL Relay by checking the server certificate against a list of trusted certificate authorities. After authentication, the client and SSL Relay perform an TLS/SSL key exchange. SSL Relay acts as a proxy by decrypting traffic before passing it to the Presentation Server. Conversely, it encrypts traffic sent back to the client.

Set Up SSL Relay

If Microsoft Certificate Authority Services is used to assist in setting up SSL Relay, the SSLAutoConfig tool can be used to simplify the process. This tool is located in the Support folder on the server installation CD. For more information about how to use SSLAutoConfig, see Advanced Concepts for Presentation Server 4.0.

Deploy SSL Relay

The following tasks are prerequisites to deploying SSL Relay:

1. Obtain a server certificate for each Presentation Server. A separate server certificate is needed for each server on which SSL Relay is intended to run. For more information on certificates, see Appendix D, "SSL/TLS Certificate Installation."

2. Install the server certificate on each server.

3. Modify the SSL Relay port number if necessary so that SSL Relay and Internet Information Services do not attempt to bind to the same port number. The port number used by Internet Information Services or SSL Relay must be changed.

Import a Certificate

SSL Relay uses Microsoft's SSL implementation, SChannel. SSL Relay uses the same registry-based certificate store as Internet Information Services. Certificates installed using Internet Information Services or the Microsoft Management Console Certificate snap-in will be available to SSL Relay. For more information on importing certificates, see Appendix D, "SSL/TLS Certificate Installation."

Change SSL Port

The Citrix SSL Relay uses TCP port 443 by default. This is the standard port for SSL connections. Optionally, SSL Relay can be configured to use another port.

NOTE Microsoft Internet Information Services also allocates port 443 for SSL connections. Configure Internet Information Services or the SSL Relay to use a different port.

IMPORTANT If the SSL Relay port is changed, the new port number must be changed in the Web Interface configuration for both Presentation Server and Program Neighborhood Agent sites. Otherwise, the Web Interface will not be able to communicate with Presentation Server.

To Set SSL Port for Internet Information Services

1. Click **Start > Programs > Administrative Tools > Internet Services Manager**.

2. In the Internet Information Services Console tree, select **Default Web Site** and choose **Properties** from the **Action** menu. The **Default Web Site Properties** dialog box appears.

3. From the **Directory Security** tab, click **Server Certificate**. The Welcome to the Web Server Certificate Wizard appears. Follow the instructions in the wizard to create or import a certificate.

4. After the server certificate is installed, select the **Web Site** tab in the **Default Web Site Properties** dialog box.

5. Change the SSL port number to something other than 443.

6. Click **OK** to close the **Default Web Site Properties** dialog box.

To Change SSL Relay Port Number

1. On the server, click the **Citrix SSL Relay Configuration Tool** button on the ICA Administrator toolbar to start the SSL Relay configuration tool.

2. On the **Connection** tab, type the new port number in the **Relay Listening Port** box.

3. Click **OK**.

4. Restart for the changes to take effect.

Refer to the *Web Interface Administrator's Guide* for the procedure to reconfigure servers that are running the Web Interface with the new port number.

IMPORTANT If the default Citrix SSL Relay port is modified, the SSLProxyHost entry in the Appsrv. ini file in the Presentation Server Client must be modified to match the new port number. For more information about client settings, see the Client for 32-Bit Windows Administrator's Guide.

Configure SSL Relay

To configure SSL Relay, do the following:

1. From the Citrix Programs group on the **Start** menu, choose **Administration Tools** and then **Citrix SSL Relay Configuration Tool** to start the SSL Relay configuration tool.

2. On the **Relay Credentials** tab, select the server certificate.

3. On the **Connection** tab, configure the fully qualified domain name (or IP address) and port combinations to which SSL Relay forwards decrypted data. SSL Relay forwards packets only to the servers and ports listed on this tab.

4. On the **Ciphersuites** tab, select which cipher suites to allow. To restrict SSL Relay to a particular set of SSL/TLS cipher suites, set the **Selected** setting to Commercial or Government, abbreviated **COM** and **GOV** in the dialog box.

   The **Commercial** value restricts connections to the following cipher suites:

   RSA_WITH_AES_128_CBC_SHA

   RSA_WITH_RC4_128_MD5

   RSA_WITH_RC4_128_SHA

   The **Government** value restricts connections to the following cipher suites:

   RSA_WITH_AES_256_CBC_SHA

   RSA_WITH_3DES_EDE_CBC_SHA

IMPORTANT   For deployments that do not use the Secure Gateway and rely on SSL Relay for secure communications, published applications must have the Enable SSL and TLS protocols check box selected. This option is available in the Client Options panel in the Published Applications properties. Note, however, that this setting does not prevent Presentation Server Clients from connecting to ICA port 1494.

Configure SecureICA

ICA encryption (Citrix SecureICA) encrypts the information sent between the Presentation Server and an ICA client. SecureICA is a proprietary encryption protocol that encrypts ICA traffic. SecureICA does not use certificates or public key cryptography. Secure ICA works by performing a Diffie Hellman key exchange between the client and the server. The result of the key exchange is two 40-, 56-, or 128-bit keys. One key is used to encrypt client-to-server communication, and the other to encrypt server-to-client communication. The RC5 encryption algorithm is used to encrypt the ICA stream. SecureICA does not provide integrity protection, replay protection, or server authentication. ICA encryption should be used in the following cases:

▼ Internal network traffic must be encrypted and end-to-end SSL/TLS is not available.

■ Communications from devices that use Microsoft DOS or run on Win16 systems must be encrypted.

■ Older devices running client software cannot be upgraded.

▲ There is little risk of man-in-the-middle attacks.

SecureICA must be enabled on both the client and the server. On the Presentation Server, the ICA encryption level is specified with the published application and can be modified in the Presentation Server Console.

Enabling SecureICA for a Published Application Using Policies   SecureICA can be enabled for specific published applications, applications, clients, or IP addresses by using Presentation Server policies. The **SecureICA encryption** policy is accessible in the **Security > Encryption** section of the **Policies**. See the section "Configuring Presentation Server Policies" for more information. The recommended **Encryption Level** is **RC5 (128-bit)**.

It is recommended that if SecureICA is required, it be enabled for all published applications using policies and not on a per-application basis. Published applications and desktops, however, require that the **Encryption** level be specified and that the **Minimum requirement** check box be selected in the **Client Options** pane in the published application properties. Otherwise, the SecureICA policy will prevent the Presentation Server Client connection from completing.

Configure Client Drive Mapping

Client drive mapping is built into the standard device redirection facilities of the Presentation Server. The client drives appear as client network objects in Windows. The client's disk drives are displayed as shared folders with mapped drive letters. Like any other network drive, these drives can be used by Windows Explorer and other applications.

Disable Client Drive Mapping

If client drive mapping is not needed, it should be disabled.

Disable Client Drive Mapping via Citrix Connection Configuration

1. In the **Citrix Connection Configuration**, right click on the **ICA-tcp** connection.

2. Click **Edit**.

3. In the **Edit Connection** window, click **Client Settings**.

4. Check the **Disable client drive mapping** check box.

5. Click **OK** to return to the **Edit Connection** window.

6. Click **OK**.

Disable Client Drive Mapping via Terminal Services Configuration

1. Click **Start > Administrative Tools > Terminal Services Configuration**.
2. In the left pane of the **Terminal Services Configuration** window, click on the **Connections** node.
3. In the right pane of the **Terminal Services Configuration** window, right click on the **ICA-tcp** connection.
4. Click **Properties**.
5. In the **ICA-tcp Properties** window, click on the **Client Settings** tab.
6. Check the **Drive mapping** check box to disable drive mapping.
7. Click **OK**.

Disable Client Drive Mapping via Policy

1. In the Presentation Server Console, select the farm in which to disable client drive mapping.
2. Right click on **Policies**.
3. In the **Policy Name** field, add a name for the policy.
4. In the **Policy Description** field, add a description for the policy.
5. Click **OK.**
6. Right click on the new policy in the **Contents** pane.
7. Click **Properties.**
8. In the **Properties** window, expand the **Client Devices** node.
9. Expand the **Resources** node.
10. Expand the **Drives** node.
11. Click **Mappings**.
12. In the **Mappings** pane, select **Enabled**.
13. Check the boxes for **Turn off Floppy disk drives**, **Turn off Hard drives**, **Turn off CD-ROM drives**, and **Turn off Remote drives** if access to these drives is not needed.
14. Click **OK**.

Configure Clipboard Mapping

Clipboard mapping is built into the standard device redirection facilities of the Presentation Server. When enabled, the ICA session's clipboard on the Presentation Server will be mapped to the Presentation Server Client. Data from the Presentation Server can be copied and pasted from the server to the client machine. When disabled, the clipboards on the server and the client will function independently, but no transfer of clipboard data will be permitted between the server and the client.

Disable Clipboard Mapping

If clipboard mapping is not needed, it should be disabled.

Disable Clipboard Mapping via Citrix Connection Configuration

1. In the **Citrix Connection Configuration**, right click on the **ICA-tcp** connection.
2. Click **Edit**.
3. In the **Edit Connection** window, click **Client Settings**.
4. Check the **Disable Client Clipboard Mapping** check box.
5. Click **OK** to return to the **Edit Connection** window.
6. Click **OK**.

Disable Clipboard Mapping via Terminal Services Configuration

1. Click **Start > Administrative Tools > Terminal Services Configuration**.
2. In the left pane of the **Terminal Services Configuration** window, click on the **Connections** node.
3. In the right pane of the **Terminal Services Configuration** window, right click on the **ICA-tcp** connection.
4. Click **Properties**.
5. In the **ICA-tcp Properties** window, click on the **Client Settings** tab.
6. Check the **Clipboard mapping** check box to disable it.
7. Click **OK**.

Disable Clipboard Mapping via Policy

1. In the Presentation Server Console, select the farm in which to disable Clipboard Mapping.
2. Right click on **Policies**.
3. In the **Policy Name** field, add a name for the policy.
4. In the **Policy Description** field, add a description for the policy.
5. Click **OK.**
6. Right click on the new policy in the **Contents** pane.
7. Click **Properties**.
8. In the **Properties** window, expand the **Client Devices** node.

9. Expand the **Resources** node.

10. Expand the **Other** node.

11. Click **Turn off clipboard mapping**.

12. In the **Turn off clipboard mapping** pane, select **Enabled**.

13. Click **OK**.

Configure Client Device Mapping

Presentation Server Clients support mapping devices on client computers so that users can access the devices within client sessions. Client device mapping provides ICA session access to the printers and serial port devices that are connected to the client machine and provides client machine access to printers and serial port devices that are connected to the server machine via the ICA session.

Disable LPT Port Mapping

If LPT port mapping is not needed, it should be disabled.

Disable LPT Port Mapping via Citrix Connection Configuration

1. In the **Citrix Connection Configuration**, right click on the **ICA-tcp** connection.

2. Click **Edit**.

3. In the **Edit Connection** window, click **Client Settings**.

4. Check the **Disable Client LPT Port Mapping** check box.

5. Click **OK** to return to the **Edit Connection** window.

6. Click **OK**.

Disable LPT Port Mapping via Terminal Services Configuration

1. Click **Start > Administrative Tools > Terminal Services Configuration**.

2. In the left pane of the **Terminal Services Configuration** window, click on the **Connections** node.

3. In the right pane of the **Terminal Services Configuration** window, right click on the **ICA-tcp** connection.

4. Click **Properties**.

5. In the **ICA-tcp Properties** window, click on the **Client Settings** tab.

6. Check the **LPT port mapping** check box.

7. Click **OK**.

Disable LPT Port Mapping via Policy

1. In the Presentation Server Console, select the farm in which to disable LPT port mapping.
2. Right click on **Policies**.
3. In the **Policy Name** field, add a name for the policy.
4. In the **Policy Description** field, add a description for the policy.
5. Click **OK.**
6. Right click on the new policy in the **Contents** pane.
7. Click **Properties**.
8. In the **Properties** window, expand the **Client Devices** node.
9. Expand the **Resources** node.
10. Expand the **Other** node.
11. Click **Turn off clipboard mapping**.
12. In the **Turn off LPT port mapping** pane, select **Enabled**.
13. Click **OK.**

Disable COM Port Mapping

If COM Port Mapping is not needed, it should be disabled.

Disable COM Port Mapping via Citrix Connection Configuration

1. In the **Citrix Connection Configuration**, right click on the **ICA-tcp** connection.
2. Click **Edit**.
3. In the **Edit Connection** window, click **Client Settings**.
4. Check the **Disable COM port mapping** check box.
5. Click **OK** to return to the **Edit Connection** window.
6. Click **OK.**

Disable COM Port Mapping via Terminal Services Configuration

1. Click **Start > Administrative Tools > Terminal Services Configuration**.
2. In the left pane of the **Terminal Services Configuration** window, click on the **Connections** node.
3. In the right pane of the **Terminal Services Configuration** window, right click on the **ICA-tcp** connection.
4. Click **Properties**.
5. In the **ICA-tcp Properties** window, click on the **Client Settings** tab.

6. Check the **COM port mapping** check box.

7. Click **OK**.

Disable COM Port Mapping via Policy

1. In the Presentation Server Console, select the farm in which to disable COM Port Mapping.

2. Right click on **Policies**.

3. In the **Policy Name** field, add a name for the policy.

4. In the **Policy Description** field, add a description for the policy.

5. Click **OK**.

6. Right click on the new policy in the **Contents** pane.

7. Click **Properties**.

8. In the **Properties** window, expand the **Client Devices** node.

9. Expand the **Resources** node.

10. Expand the **Other** node.

11. Click **Turn off COM port mapping**.

12. In the **Turn off COM port mapping** pane, select **Enabled**.

13. Click **OK**.

Secure the IMA Data Store

The data store can be configured to use a number of different back-end SQL database servers. The most basic option is for the data store to be stored by using Microsoft Access in a local database. Microsoft SQL Server Desktop Edition, Microsoft SQL Server, IBM DB2, and Oracle also are supported. It important to secure the network connection to the SQL server by using IPsec or SSL/TLS if the data store database back end is not installed on the dedicated Presentation Server data store server. A dedicated data store user has to be created on the database back end.

Microsoft Access

If a Microsoft Access database was chosen during installation, the default password must be changed. During installation the access data store was created with a default username of "**citrix**" and the password "**citrix**". These access credentials should be changed by using the **dsmaint** configuration tool.

Microsoft SQL Server

Configure Microsoft SQL Server to use Windows integrated authentication. Create a new user to be employed to access the data store. After the database has been created, remove the **db_owner** permission from the user. The user account will need only **db_reader** and **db_writer** permissions to the data store. This prevents the user from being able to remove the data store's database altogether if the account was compromised.

IBM DB2

The DB2 user account that is to be used to access the data store needs only the following DB2 permissions:

▼   Connect database

■   Create tables

▲   Create schemas implicitly

Once the account has been created, update the user name and password to be used by IMA, using the **dsmaint** configuration tool.

Oracle

The Oracle user account to be used needs only the **connect** and **resource** permissions. The systems access (SA) account permissions should be removed.

Using Dsmaint

Dsmaint is an administration tool that modifies the parameters IMA uses to connect to the datastore. It is available only to and can be run only by Citrix administrators. Any time the SQL server credentials are modified, the new values must be made available to IMA. The **dsmaint** configuration tool is used to set the credentials in IMA. To change the SQL credentials run **dsmaint** as follows:

```
dsmaint config [/user:<username>] [/pwd:<password>] [</dsn:<filename>]
```

When an Access database is used, run **dsmaint** as follows:

```
dsmaint config /pwd:<password> /dsn:<filename>
```

Configure Citrix Administrator Accounts

Citrix administrators are individuals tasked with managing server farms. Citrix administrator accounts can have the following privilege levels:

▼   *Full.* Full Citrix administrators can manage all aspects of a server farm. They can, for example, publish applications, manage printers, terminate user sessions, and create other Citrix administrator accounts.

■   *View only.* View-only Citrix administrators can view all aspects of the server farm; they can, for example, view configuration information and monitor session states, but they cannot modify any settings.

▲   *Custom.* Custom Citrix administrators can perform select, limited sets of tasks.

To give Citrix administrators of a server farm access to the Presentation Server Console, add their user accounts to the Citrix Administrators group. The console uses standard Windows network logon and user account authentication mechanisms. Click the Citrix Administrator node in the left pane of the console to view all Citrix administrators.

> *NOTE*   To create, delete, and configure Citrix administrator accounts, log on to the Presentation Server Console as a full administration Citrix administrator.

The privilege level granted to a Citrix administrator should depend on the specific business function of that administrator. For example, system or network Citrix administrators may need complete access to most areas of farm management, whereas help desk personnel may need only view-only access to particular areas.

Grant Only the Minimum Level of Privilege   To minimize the impact of an attack by a rogue administrator, do not designate Citrix administrators to be privileged Windows users. Privileged Windows users include administrators, power users, and any other users who have been granted special privileges or permissions. Grant Citrix administrators permission only for the tasks they need to perform their job functions by using the **Custom** level of Citrix administrator privileges.

To Create Citrix Administrator Accounts

1. In the Presentation Server Console, from the Actions menu, select **New > MetaFrame Administrator**. The first page of the **Add MetaFrame Administrator** Wizard appears.

2. In the **Look in** list, select the user or user group accounts to add to the Citrix Administrators group and then click **Add**. Select **Show Users** to display all user names in the selected domain.

3. Click **Next**.

4. On the **Privileges** page, select the privilege level to grant the selected Citrix administrator accounts. Select among the following options:

   Select **View Only** to give the selected Citrix administrators view-only access to all areas of farm management. Click **Finish**.

   Select **Full Administration** to give the selected Citrix administrators full access to all areas of farm management. Click **Finish**.

   Select **Custom** to delegate specific, limited tasks to the selected Citrix administrators. Click **Next** when finished and proceed to step 5.

5. On the **Permissions** page, in the **Folders** pane, select the folder or node to delegate the corresponding tasks to the selected Citrix administrators. The tasks that can be delegated for the selected node or folder appear in the **Tasks** pane.

6. In the **Tasks** pane, select the tasks to delegate.

7. Click **Finish**.

Delegate Tasks to Custom Citrix Administrators Tasks can be delegated to custom Citrix administrator accounts during Citrix administrator creation or by editing an existing Citrix administrator account's properties. Tasks are delegated by associating custom Citrix administrator accounts with permissions to perform select tasks.

Permissions that are set on nodes (Policies, Printer Management, and so on) apply farmwide. Permissions that are set on folders (Applications, Servers, and any folders within) apply only to the applications and servers contained within the selected folder.

Permissions cannot be granted to applications and servers directly. For permissions to be granted to applications or servers, they must be placed in folders, and then permission can be granted at the folder level.

 NOTE Only full administration Citrix administrators can create, delete, and configure Citrix administrator accounts.

To Associate an Citrix Administrator Account with Select Tasks

1. In the left pane of the Presentation Server Console, select **Citrix Administrators**. The list of configured Citrix administrator accounts appears in the **Contents** tab.

2. In the **Contents** tab, select the Citrix administrator account to delegate a task or tasks to and choose **Properties** from the **Actions** menu. The **Properties** page for the selected Citrix administrator account appears.

3. If the Citrix administrator is not a custom Citrix administrator, on the **Properties** page select **Privilege Type and** then select the **Custom** option.

4. On the **Properties** page, select **Permissions**. The **Permissions** page appears, featuring the **Folders** and **Tasks** panes.

5. In the **Folders** pane, select the folder or node to delegate tasks to the selected Citrix administrator. The tasks associated with the selected folder or node appear in the **Tasks** pane.

6. In the **Tasks** pane, select the tasks to delegate.

7. Click **OK**.

Configure Citrix Connection Configuration

 NOTE The Citrix Connection Configuration tool is used only for configuring Presentation Server 4.0 on 32-bit Windows. For the Presentation Server 4.0 on 64-bit Windows and later versions of the Presentation Server, refer to the section "Configure Terminal Services Configuration."

Independent of the Presentation Server Console, settings can be configured for ICA sessions by using the Citrix Connection Configuration utility.

To Configure Citrix Connection Configuration

1. In the **Citrix Connection Configuration**, right click on the **ICA-tcp** connection.

2. Click **Edit**.

3. In the **Edit Connection** window, click **Client Settings**.

4. In the **Client Mapping Overrides** section, check the following checkboxes if the particular client mapping is not needed:

   ■ Disable Client Drive Mapping

   ■ Disable Windows Client Printer Mapping

   ■ Disable Client LPT Port Mapping

   ■ Disable Client COM Port Mapping

   ■ Disable Client Clipboard Mapping

   ■ Disable Client Audio Mapping

5. Click **OK**.

6. In the **Edit Connection** window, click **Advanced**.

7. In the **Security** section, select **RC5 (128 bit)** to encrypt the ICA session network traffic with SecureICA. Select this if ICA sessions are not protected by SSL/TLS or a VPN.

8. In the **Initial Program** section, check the **(inherit client/user config)** check box. Next, check the **Only launch Published Applications** check box. Select this setting to ensure that users can launch only published applications.

9. Click **OK** to return to the **Edit Connection** window.

10. Click **OK**.

Configure Terminal Services Configuration

NOTE The Terminal Services Configuration tool is used only for configuring Presentation Server 4.0 on 64-bit Windows and later versions of Presentation Server 4.0. For Presentation Server 4.0 on 32-bit Windows, refer to the section "Configure Citrix Connection Configuration."

Independent of the Presentation Server Console, settings can be configured for ICA sessions by using the Terminal Services Configuration utility.

To Configure Terminal Services Configuration

1. Click **Start > Administrative Tools > Terminal Services Configuration**.

2. In the left pane of the **Terminal Services Configuration** window, click on the **Connections** node.

3. In the right pane of the **Terminal Services Configuration** window, right click on the **ICA-tcp** connection.

4. Click **Properties**.

5. In the **ICA-tcp Properties** window, click the **Client Settings** tab.

6. Check the following check boxes for client mappings if they are not needed:

   ■ Drive mapping

   ■ Windows printer mapping

   ■ LPT port mapping

   ■ COM port mapping

   ■ Clipboard mapping

   ■ Audio mapping

7. Click the **ICA Settings** tab.

8. In the **Initial Program** section, check the **Non-administrators can only launch published desktops** check box. Enable this setting to ensure that users can launch only published applications.

9. Click **OK**.

Configure Presentation Server Policies

Policies can be used to apply select settings to connections filtered for specific users, client devices, IP addresses, or servers. The use of policies is an efficient method for controlling security settings for groups of users, clients, and servers.

Policies contain rules that define their settings. A single policy can apply multiple rules. Policies also can contain rules that are not used for security enforcement. These policies are not discussed in this book.

Policies are applied when users log on to the server farm and remain in effect for the length of a user's session. In general, policies override similar settings configured for the entire server farm, for specific servers, or on the client. However, the highest encryption setting and the most restrictive shadowing setting always override other settings.

Policy rules have three states: enabled, disabled, and not configured. By default, all rules are not configured. All unconfigured rules are ignored when users log on to the server, and so the rules come into play only when the state is enabled or disabled.

Create Policies

The basic steps for effectively creating and using policies are as follows. These steps are explained in more detail below.

1. Decide on the criteria on which to base the policies.

2. Create the policy. Creating a policy involves the following steps:

- Naming the policy
- Assigning the policy to user accounts, client devices, or servers
- Setting the policy's rules

3. Prioritize policies.

Policies can be prioritized to set the order in which they take priority over one another when they contain conflicting rules. Higher-priority policies take precedence over lower-priority policies.

In creating policies for groups of users, clients, or servers, some members of the group may require exceptions to some policy rules. To manage exceptions more effectively, new policies can be created for only those group members who need the exceptions. These policies should be prioritized higher than the policy for the entire group.

To Create a Policy

1. In the Presentation Server Console, select the Policies node in the left pane and choose **Actions > New > Policy** or click the **Create Policy** button on the console toolbar.

2. In the **New Policy** dialog box, enter the name and description of the policy and then click **OK**.

Examples of policy names are "Accounting Department" and "Lender Laptops." The policy name is displayed in the right pane of the console. After a policy is created, at least one filter must be configured that determines the sessions to which that policy applies.

Configure Policy Rules

Policy rules can be used to configure the connection settings that will be applied when a policy is enforced. Policies can contain multiple rules. Policy rules have three states: enabled, disabled, and not configured. By default, not all rules are configured. All rules that are not configured are ignored when users log on to the server, and so the rules come into play only when the state is enabled or disabled.

To Configure Policy Rules

1. The policy's rules can be set on the policy's property sheet. Select the policy and choose **Actions > Properties** to open its property sheet. Some policy rules are organized into folders. Expand the folders to view the rules that can be applied.

2. When setting policy rules, determine which settings to apply. For any rule that is to be added to the policy, select **Enabled** and set rule options in the right pane. For more information about policy rules, select the rule in question and then click **Help**.

3. Click **OK**.

Override Policies

Policies are applied when users log on and remain in effect for the length of the session. In general, connection policies override similar settings configured for the entire server farm, for specific servers, or on the client. However, the highest encryption setting and the most restrictive shadowing setting always override other settings.

IMPORTANT   Microsoft Group Policy settings can override Presentation Server policy rules if the Microsoft Group Policy settings are more restrictive. If the connection behavior does not match the expected results, check the Microsoft Group Policy settings for conflicting configurations.

Create Exceptions to Policies   After basic policies are created using the organization's primary criteria, additional policies may be needed for individual users or groups of users that require exceptions to some policy rules. For example, additional restrictions could be placed on users who should not be permitted to access their client drives. A policy can be created that disables clients' drive mapping for their ICA sessions.

However, if some of the people in the user group should not need access to their local drives, another policy can be created for only those users to disable client drive mapping. The two policies can be prioritized to control which one should take precedence.

Prioritizing Policies

Policies can be prioritized by setting the priority number. By default, new policies are given the lowest priority. In cases of conflicting policy settings, a policy with a higher priority will override a policy with a lower priority. A policy with the priority number of 1 has the highest priority. If there are five policies prioritized 1 through 5, the policy prioritized with priority number 5 has the lowest priority. In the following procedure, the interwoven example assumes that a policy was created for an "Accounting" user group. One of the rules enabled in this policy prevents the user group from saving data to its local drives. However, two users who are members of the Accounting group travel to remote offices to perform audits and need to save data to their local drives.

The steps below describe the process of creating a new policy for Accounting group members Carol and Martin that will give them access to their local drives while allowing the other policy rules to work the same way for them as for all the other members of the Accounting group.

1. Determine which users need additional policies to create exceptions. The policy named "Accounting Profile" that is assigned to the Accounting group includes a rule that prevents access to local drives. Carol and Martin, members of the Accounting group, need access to their local drives.

2. Determine which rule or rules should not apply to these users. For example, most of the rules in this policy should apply at all times to all users, with the exception of the rule that prevents access to local drives.

3. Create a new policy. Refer to the earlier section "To Create a Policy" for more information. For this example, name this policy "Accounting Profile—local drive access."

4. Edit the description of the policy by selecting the policy and choosing **Actions > Policy > Edit Description**. Use policy descriptions to help keep track of the policies.

5. Open the policy's property sheet and locate the rule that should not to apply to Carol and Martin. Set the rule's state to **Disabled**.

6. To assign users Carol and Martin to the policy, select it and choose **Actions > Policy > Apply this policy to**. In the **Policy Filters** dialog box, select **Users** and make sure the **Filter based on users** check box is selected. Open domains or user groups in the **Look in** box until the user accounts for Carol and Martin are displayed and then add them to the **Configured Accounts** box. Select the **Show Users** option to display individual user accounts.

7. Click **OK** to finish adding users.

8. Prioritize the "Accounting Profile—local drive access" policy higher than the "Accounting Profile" policy. By default, new policies are given the lowest priority (which corresponds to the highest priority number). Right click the "Accounting Profile—local drive access" policy and select **Priority > Increase Priority** until this policy's priority number is lower than that of the "Accounting Profile" policy. A policy with a priority number of 1 has the highest priority.

When a user logs on, all policies that match the filters for the connection are identified. The Presentation Server sorts the identified policies into priority order and compares multiple instances of any rule, applying the rule according to the priority. If the rule appears in a policy prioritized the highest, those rule settings will override the settings for the same rule in a policy that is prioritized lower.

Any rule configured as disabled wins over a lower-priority rule that is enabled. Similarly, any rule configured as enabled wins over a lower-priority rule that is disabled. Policy rules that are not configured are ignored and will not override the settings of lower-priority rules.

Apply a Policy

By default, newly created policies are not applied to any sessions. Before a policy has an effect, a filter for it must be created so that the server can apply it to matching sessions. Sessions can be filtered and have policies applied to them to them on the basis of a combination of the following criteria:

▼ IP address of a client device connecting to a session

■ Name of a client device connecting to a session

■ Users or user groups associated with a session

▲ Server hosting a session

When both user group and client device filters are applied, one policy can be created for the employees in a New York office when they connect from their office workstations and another policy can be created for the same New York employees that sets a higher encryption level for sessions connecting from the laptops that the employees use in the field.

Appropriate Use of a Client Name   Policies can be filtered on the basis of the name of a client device. Although this filtering works in the described manner, it should be noted that the name of the client device is a string value that can be configured manually on the client host.

As the client device name can be set to an arbitrary value by the client, it may not always be appropriate to base policy filtering decisions on this value. In cases where the client should not be permitted to influence the policy filtering, it may not be appropriate to make use of the client device name.

In addition, for some versions of Web Interface, using a value of WI_* for the client name filter can be done to assign a policy to all users accessing applications through the Web Interface. Policies that filter on the basis of client name will work as described, but administrators should be aware that clients may be able to manually configure the name of the client device and set it to a value that may or may not match the above wildcard.

To Apply a Policy

1. In the left pane of the console, choose the **Policies** node.

2. In the **Contents** tab, choose the policy to apply.

3. From the **Actions** menu, choose **Policy > Apply this policy to**.

4. Use the **Policy Filters** dialog box to configure filters to apply the policy to a session based on client IP address, client name, the server the session connects to, or the user who is making the connection.

   ■ To apply the policy to client IP addresses, click **Client IP Address** in the left pane and select **Filter based on client IP address**. Click **Add** to configure an individual address or range of addresses and then specify whether to allow or deny the addresses for the policy.

   ■ To apply the policy to client names, click **Client Name** in the left pane and select **Filter based on client name**. Click **Add** to specify a client name to which the policy applies.

IMPORTANT   Client names should not be used as a filter unless they can be trusted for that purpose.

   ■ To apply the policy to servers, click **Servers** in the left pane and select **Filter based on servers**. Select servers or folders of servers in the right pane and choose to apply or not apply the policy to them.

- To apply the policy to users, click **Users** in the left pane and select **Filter based on users**. Select the user group and/or users to whom the policy is to be assigned and then click **Add**.

  By default, the policy is allowed for any users or user groups added to the configured accounts list. If there are members of the user group who should not be assigned to this policy, add those individual members of the group and then select **Deny** to prevent the policy from being applied to them.

5. If a filter has an **Allow/Deny** setting, select **Allow** to enforce the policy.

6. Click **OK** to finish applying the policy filters.

NOTE To assign policies to all users accessing applications through the Web Interface, use the wildcard expression WI_* when specifying the client name filter. Users accessing applications through the Web Interface receive a random client name of WI_number, where the number is random ASCII characters.

Searching for Policies and Viewing Results of Multiple Policies

To find policies and determine the effective rule settings when more than one policy applies to a session, use **Search**. Search can be used to list policies that apply to a connection based on

▼ The IP address of the client device making the connection

■ The name of the client device making the connection

■ The user or group membership of the user making the connection

▲ The server to which the connection is being made

To Use Search for Policies

1. Make sure that **Policies** is the selected entry in the **Search for** list. Search finds all policies that apply to the combination of access control, IP address, client name, user, and server criteria specified in the **Search** dialog box.

2. Use the **View Resultant Policy** function after a policy search to calculate the results of multiple policies that can affect a connection. Presentation Server merges all policies that can affect a connection when enforcing policies.

When there are multiple policies that can apply to a connection, it is the resultant policy that the Presentation Server enforces.

Configure Group Policy for the Presentation Server

It may be necessary to set various policies to ensure that the servers meet the organization's security requirements. These policies can be set in each individual server's Local

Security Policy or for groups of servers by using the active directory. The following policies are recommended for the Presentation Server.

Configure Group Policies in Active Directory

In applying policies via the active directory, put the Presentation Server machines in a separate OU so that unintended settings are not applied to them.

To Configure Group Policy in Active Directory

1. Log on to the server as an administrator and start the MMC (**Start > Run type mmc** and click **OK**). The **Console1** window appears.

2. From the File menu, click **Add/Remove Snap-in**. At the **Add/Remove Snapin** dialog box, click **Add**. Select **Group Policy Object Editor** and click **Add**.

3. At the **Select Group Policy Object** dialog box, click **Browse**.

4. At the **Browse for a Group Policy Object** dialog box, click the new policy icon. A policy entry is added to the list. Enter the policy name, for example, MyPolicy, and click **OK**.

5. The new policy is shown in the **Select Group Policy Object** dialog box. Click **Finish**. Click **Close** and then click **OK**. The new group policy appears in the **Console Root** window.

6. Right click the new policy and select **Properties**. At the dialog box, select the **Security** tab.

7. Select the **Domain Admins** group and ensure that **Apply Group Policy** permission is set to **Deny**. Repeat this step for the enterprise admins group (for example, **Enterprise Admins**).

8. Add the required user groups (for example, **Domain Users**). Click **Add**. The **Select Users, Computers, or Groups** dialog box appears. Type **Domain Users** in the **Enter the object names to select** box and click **OK**.

9. Select the user group (for example, **Domain Users**) and ensure that **Apply Group Policy** is set to **Allow**. This ensures that the group policy applies to the user group. Click **OK**. A **Security** dialog box appears. The dialog box confirms that Deny entries take priority over Allow entries. This is required in the Common Criteria evaluated deployment to ensure that the group policy is not applied to the administrator groups. Click **Yes**.

10. Select the new group policy and configure the policy settings as detailed in the steps described in the sections "Computer Configuration" and "User Configuration."

Computer Configuration   Omitted items should be set in accordance with the organization's internal policies. The following are recommended settings in a Presentation Server environment.

1. Navigate to **Computer Configuration > Windows Settings > Security Settings > Local Policies > User Rights Assignment**. Set the following:

Policy	Computer Setting
Allow logon through Terminal Services	Remote desktop users Administrators
Deny access to this computer from the network	Anonymous logon Guest Support
Deny logon locally	Support Remote desktop users
Deny logon through Terminal Services	Service

2. Navigate to **Computer Configuration > Windows Settings > Security Settings > Local Policies > Security Options**. Set the following:

Policy	Computer Setting
Accounts: Limit local account use of blank passwords to console logon only	Enabled
Devices: Prevent users from installing printer drivers	Enabled
Devices: Restrict CD-ROM access to locally logged-on user only	Enabled
Devices: Restrict floppy access to locally logged-on user only	Enabled
Network access: Do not allow anonymous enumeration of SAM accounts	Enabled
Network access: Do not allow storage of credentials or .NET passports for network authentication	Enabled
Shutdown: Allow system to be shut down without having to log on	Disabled

3. Navigate to **Computer Configuration > Administrative Templates > System > Internet Communication Management**. Set the following:

Policy	Computer Setting
Restrict Internet communication	Enabled

4. Navigate to **Computer Configuration > Administrative Templates > Printers**. Set the following:

Policy	Computer Setting
Allow Printers to be published	Disabled

The following local machine policies also can be configured in the **Computer Configuration** panel. These policy settings should be configured according to the organization's internal policies.

▼ Password

■ Account Lockout

■ Event Log

■ Internet Explorer

■ Remote Assistance

▲ Internet Communication Management

User Configuration

1. Navigate to **User Configuration > Administrative Templates > Windows Components > Internet Explorer**. Set the following:

Policy	Computer Setting
Disable Save this program to disk option	Enabled

2. Navigate to **User Configuration > Administrative Templates > Windows Components > Windows Explorer > Browser Menus**. Set the following:

Policy	Computer Setting
Removes Folder Options menu item from Tools menu	Enabled
Remove File menu from Windows Explorer	Enabled
Remove "Map Network Drive" and "Disconnect Network Drive"	Enabled
Remove Search button from Windows Explorer	Enabled

Policy	Computer Setting
Remove Windows Explorer's default context menu	Enabled
Hides the Manage item on the Windows Explorer context menu	Enabled
Hide these specified drives in My Computer	Enabled; restrict A, B, C, and D drives
Prevent access to drives from My Computer	Enabled; restrict A, B, C, and D drives
	NOTE *This assumes that A, B, C, and D are all server side drives that the client does not need to access.*
Remove Hardware tab	Enabled
No "Computers Near Me" in My Network Places	Enabled
No "Entire Network" in My Network Places	Enabled
In the folder "Common Open File Dialog," hide the common dialog places bar	Enabled

3. Navigate to **User Configuration > Administrative Templates > Windows Components > Microsoft Management Console**. Set the following:

Policy	Computer Setting
Restrict the user from entering author mode	Enabled

4. Navigate to **User Configuration > Administrative Templates > Windows Components > Task Scheduler**. Set the following:

Policy	Computer Setting
Prevent Task Run or End	Enabled
Prohibit New Task Creation	Enabled
Prohibit Task Deletion	Enabled

5. Navigate to **User Configuration > Administrative Templates > Windows Components > Windows Update**. Set the following, as shown next.

Policy	Computer Setting
Remove access to use all Windows Update features	Enabled

6. Navigate to **User Configuration > Administrative Templates > Control Panel**. Set the following:

Policy	Computer Setting
Prohibit access to Control Panel	Enabled

7. Navigate to **User Configuration > Administrative Templates > Control Panel > Printers**. Set the following:

Policy	Computer Setting
Prevent addition of printers	Enabled

8. Navigate to **User Configuration > Administrative Templates > System**. Set the following:

Policy	Computer Setting
Prevent access to registry editing tools	Enabled
	Also, set "Disable regedit from running silently?" to yes.
Turn off Autoplay	Enabled, all drives
Download missing COM components	Disabled

9. Close the MMC **Console1** window and restart the Presentation Server.

Note that many of the settings related to **User Configuration > Administrative Templates > Start Menu and Taskbar** and **User Configuration > Administrative Templates > System > Ctrl+Alt+Del Options** are dependent on the types of applications published to the users and what the role of a user is. For example, certain users may need full remote desktops whereas others need access only to published applications.

Set Group Policy Priority   After the domainwide group policies have been defined, they must be enabled as the primary policies on the targeted Presentation Servers. It is necessary to ensure that other group policies do not override the created deployment policy. Note that it is recommended to create slightly different policies for Presentation Servers that have different roles. The Presentation Server roles are determined by the particular deployment scenario chosen.

1. Log on to the server as a Windows administrator.

2. Launch the Local Security Settings (**Start > Settings > Control Panel > Administrative Tools > Local Security Policy**).

3. The **Active Directory Users and Computers** window appears. Select the domain from the tree view and click **Action > Properties**. The **Properties** dialog box appears.

4. Select the **Group Policy** tab, select the saved deployment policy, and click **Up** until the policy appears at the top of the list.

5. Click **OK** to accept the change and close the **Properties** dialog box. Close the **Active Directory Users and Computers** window.

Secure the SNMP Configuration

The Simple Network Management Protocol (SNMP) is available on Windows Server 2003 as a stand-alone service. Citrix provides a plug-in Data Link Layer (DLL) to the Windows SNMP service that exposes the Citrix Management Information Base (MIB). Windows Server 2003 by default accepts SNMP messages only from the local host.

IMPORTANT The Microsoft Security Configuration Wizard must have the SNMP services listed as an approved service.

To Secure SNMP Configuration

1. Right click on **My Computer**. Select **Manage**.

2. Double click on **Services and Applications**.

3. Double click on **Services**.

4. Locate the **SNMP Service**.

5. Right **click** and locate the **Security** tab.

6. Modify the **Community String** to a unique value.

7. Add the list of hosts that are allowed to query values from the SNMP service.

8. Close the dialog box.

9. Restart the SNMP service.

Secure IMA Communication

IMA enables a Presentation Server farm to maintain configuration consistency. To ensure consistency, IMA must communicate with other IMA servers in the farm and the data store. The data store holds all the configuration and published application settings in the farm. This information is pushed out to other servers in the farm via IMA. By default, IMA communicates with other IMA servers over TCP port 2512.

IMA servers do not perform strong authentication. It is necessary to segment a Presentation Server farm away from other networks. At minimum, the IMA port should not be reachable from outside the farm. Intrafarm communication can be secured further by using IPsec or another secure communications solution. The configuration of IPsec is beyond the scope of this book.

Access the Presentation Server Console Only as a Published Application

The Presentation Server Console communicates with the Presentation Server over TCP port 2513. This port should not be available from outside the Presentation Server farm. The Presentation Server Console should be made available as a published application on the Presentation Server. By publishing the Presentation Server Console and connecting the console only to the Presentation Server that it is published on, the Citrix administrator credentials will not be transmitted over the network. If the Presentation Server Console must connect remotely, it is recommended that the connection to the Presentation Server be secured using IPsec.

IMPORTANT   The Presentation Server Console should be published only for Citrix administrators.

Access the Access Suite Console Only as a Published Application

The Access Suite Console communicates with the Presentation Server by using COM+. COM applications use Remote Procedure Calls (RPCs) to communicate over the network. This forces restrictions on the part of the enterprise network from which the Access Suite Console can be run. The RPC calls between Presentation Servers are secured using RPC packet privacy. The Presentation Server farm should not be remotely administered; the RPC port should be blocked by the firewall that shields the Presentation Server farm. The Access Suite Console should be available as a published application.

IMPORTANT   The Access Suite Console should be published only for Citrix administrators.

NOTE The RPC endpoint mapping service uses port 135 for RPC connections. In addition, a dynamic port range is used. The default port range for the dynamic ports is TCP port 1024-65535.

Secure Printer Connections

The Presentation Server supports client printers, server printers, and network printers. Printers, print management, and print driver management are configured through user policies on the Presentation Server. If the Presentation Server clients do not require access to printers, printing support should be disabled. To disable printing support in Presentation Server, see the steps in the section "Configure Group Policy for Presentation Server."

When printer support is required, the supported print scenarios must be determined. These scenarios can be a combination of any of the following:

▼ *Client printers.* A client printer is a printer attached to the Presentation Server Client device. This printer is made available to the client user's published applications that are running on the Presentation Server.

■ *Server printers.* A server printer is a printer that is attached to the Presentation Server. This printer can be made available to the Presentation Server sessions.

▲ *Network printers.* Network printers are remote printers that are reachable by either the Presentation Server Client or the Presentation Server. These printers are different from client printers because the Presentation Server can be configured to attempt a direct connection to the printer rather than going through the client.

Printers are configured via policies in the Presentation Server Console.

Disable Client Printer Mapping via Policy

1. In the Presentation Server Console, select the farm to disable client printer mapping.
2. Right click on **Policies**.
3. In the **Policy Name** field, add a name for the policy.
4. In the **Policy Description** field, add a description for the policy.
5. Click **OK**.
6. Right click on the new policy in the **Contents** pane.
7. Click **Properties**.
8. In the **Properties** window, expand the **Printing** node.
9. Expand the **Client Printers** node.
10. Click **Turn off client printer mapping**.
11. In the **Mappings** pane, select **Enabled**.
12. Click **OK**.

Disable Session Printers via Policy

1. In the Presentation Server Console, select the farm to disable client printer mapping.

2. Right click on **Policies**.

3. In the **Policy Name** field, add a name for the policy.

4. In the **Policy Description** field, add a description for the policy.

5. Click **OK**.

6. Right click on the new policy in the **Contents** pane.

7. Click **Properties**.

8. In the **Properties** window, expand the **Printing** node.

9. Click **Session printers**.

10. In the **Session printers** pane, select **Enabled**.

11. Click **OK**.

Printer policies can be applied selectively to criteria that include username, group membership, and IP address. For more information, refer to the section "Configure Presentation Server Policies."

Secure Installation Manager Deployments

▼ An account for executing the packager. If ADF packages have to be deployed, this account must be a member of the administrators group. This account should exist only on the ADF staging machine. IM also can deploy MSI and MSM files.

■ An account for copying packages to the network share point server. This account must have read and write user rights to the network.

▲ An account for retrieving packages from the network share point and the installation of these packages on target servers. This account is specified in the console. The ADF staging machine should be a "clean" dedicated Presentation Server that does not have any other roles. Minimize the amount of software installed on this server and do not allow Presentation Server clients to connect to the server.

Finally, both the Installation Manager staging machine and the network share that contains the package to be deployed should be accessible only from within the Presentation Server farm. One way to do this is to disable Windows file and printer sharing (SMB Protocol) at the firewall; this limits access to the Presentation Server farm from the rest of the enterprise network.

Secure the XML Service and Secure Ticket Authority

The XML service can run by itself or as a component within Microsoft's Internet Information Services. The Secure Ticket Authority is a component of the XML service. Access to the XML service and STA can be restricted to specific IP address ranges. The XML service also can be hosted by the XTE Server if Internet Information Services is not available.

One Presentation Server should be designated as the "primary" Presentation Server and used to run the XML service and the STA. This server will be responsible for communicating with the Web Interface if the Web Interface is running on a separate machine.

Both the XML service communication and Secure Ticket Authority communication should be secured with IPsec or SSL/TLS. The XML service listening port number may have to be modified. Consult the *Presentation Server Administrator's Guide* for instructions on modifying the XML service port number.

IMPORTANT   All servers in the farm must use the same port for the Citrix XML service.

When the XML service is set to share its port with Internet Information Services, ensure that Internet Information Services is configured for HTTPS traffic only.

Secure Ticket Authority Log

After the installation and configuration of the Presentation Server on the primary server, the default directory in which the Secure Ticket Authority logs are stored must be changed so that unauthorized users cannot view Secure Ticket Authority logs. Access also must be restricted to the Secure Ticket Authority, and a log directory must be specified. When the Secure Ticket Authority is running inside Internet Information Services, modify the configuration file as follows.

To Change the Secure Ticket Authority Log Directory

1. Create a new directory, C:\citrixlogs\stalog.
2. Open the CtxSta.config file stored in C:\Inetpub\Scripts. Amend the LogDir line in the file to read

    ```
    LogDir=C:\citrixlogs\stalog\
    ```

3. Save the changes and close the file.
4. Remove read access to the STA log directory from normal users. Only the account running IIS and the Windows Administrator should have access to the directory.

Restricting Access to XML Service and STA

It is necessary to restrict access to the XML service. Access to the XML service and the STA can be configured separately. For example, when the XML service is running within

Internet Information Services, it is possible to restrict access to the service by IP addresses and domain names. This is accomplished by configuring restrictions within Internet Information Services. Access to the STA can be restricted even when Internet Information Services is not used by editing the STA configuration file, CtxSta.config.

To Restrict Access to Secure Ticket Authority and XML Service with Internet Information Services

1. Launch the Internet Information Services Manager (**Start > All Programs > Administrative Tools > Internet Information Services (IIS) Manager**).

2. From the Internet Information Services tree view, expand and select **primary server computer name (local computer) > Web Sites > Default Web Site > Scripts**.

3. Right click ctxsta.dll and select **Properties**.

4. At the ctxsta.dll **Properties** dialog box, select the **File Security** tab.

5. In the IP address and domain name restrictions section, click **Edit**.

6. In the **IP Address** and **Domain Name Restrictions** dialog box, select **Denied Access**.

7. Click **Add**. At the **Grant Access** dialog box, select **Single Computer** and enter the IP address for the Web Interface server. Click **OK**.

8. Click **Add**. At the **Grant Access** dialog box, select **Single Computer** and enter the IP address for the Secure Gateway server. Click **OK**.

9. In the **IP Address and Domain Name Restrictions** dialog box, click **OK**.

10. Back in the ctxsta.dll **Properties** dialog box, click **OK**.

11. Right click wpnbr.dll and select **Properties**.

12. At the wpnbr.dll **Properties** dialog box, select the **File Security** tab.

13. In the IP address and domain name restrictions section, click **Edit**.

14. In the **IP Address** and **Domain Name Restrictions** dialog box, select **Denied Access**.

15. Click **Add**. In the **Grant Access** dialog box, select **Single Computer,** and enter the IP address for the Web Interface server. Click **OK**.

16. In the **IP Address and Domain Name Restrictions** dialog box, click **OK**.

17. Back in the wpnbr.dll **Properties** dialog box, click **OK**.

18. **Close** the Internet Information Services (IIS) Manager window.

IMPORTANT   It may be necessary to add the Presentation Server local IP address to the IP filter list created within Internet Information Services.

To Restrict Access to Secure Ticket Authority Without Internet Information Services

1. Open the file CtxSta.config file stored in C:\Program Files\Citrix\System32. The file will look like the following:

```
LogDir=C:\citrixlogs\stalog\

; Allowed Client IP addresses

; To change, substitute * with client IP addresses.

; Use ";" to separate IP addresses/address ranges.

; To specify a range of IPs always use StartIP-EndIP.

; For example, AllowedClientIPList=192.168.1.1;10.8.1.12-
10.8.1.18;123.1.2.3

AllowedClientIPList=*

; SSL only mode

; If set to on, only requests sent through HTTPS are accepted

SSLOnly=off
```

2. Modify the **AllowedClientIPList** to match the IP addresses of the Web Interface servers, the local IP address of the Presentation Server, and the IP address of the Secure Gateway Server.
3. Enable **SSLOnly=on** if SSL is required.
4. Save the file and reboot the server for the changes to take effect.

Only Launch Published Applications

Connection settings are restricted by default to allow sessions to open only with a published application as configured by an administrator. This restriction ensures, for example, that users cannot create custom connections to launch a session with a desktop or arbitrary application on the server to which they are not permitted access.

Restrict Connections via Citrix Connection Configuration

1. In the **Citrix Connection Configuration**, right click on the **ICA-tcp** connection.
2. Click **Edit**.
3. In the **Edit Connection** window, click **Advanced**.

4. In the **Initial Program** section, check the **(inherit client/user config)** check box. Next, check the **Only launch Published Applications** check box. Select this setting to ensure that users can launch only published applications.

5. Click **OK** to return to the **Edit Connection** window.

6. Click **OK**.

Restrict Connections via Terminal Services Configuration

1. Click **Start > Administrative Tools > Terminal Services Configuration**.

2. In the left pane of the **Terminal Services Configuration** window, click on the **Connections** node.

3. In the right pane of the **Terminal Services Configuration** window, right click on the **ICA-tcp** connection.

4. Click **Properties**.

5. Click the **ICA Settings** tab.

6. In the **Initial Program** section, check the **Non-administrators can only launch published desktops** check box. Enable this setting to ensure that users can launch only published applications.

7. Click **OK**.

This setting does not apply to administrators. Administrators can, for example, launch a server desktop as the initial program of a connection even if the desktop is not a published resource and **Only launch Published Applications** is selected.

Secure the Pass-Through Client

To secure the Pass-Through Client, refer to Chapter 8, "Presentation Server Client."

Run Published Applications Only as a Nonprivileged User

To minimize the impact of an attack on the Presentation Server, do not run any published applications as a privileged user. Privileged users include administrators, power users, and any other users who have been granted special privileges or permissions. Instead, run the published application under a regular, nonprivileged user account that is not in the administrators group. This will limit the impact to the Presentation Server if the published application or ICA session is attacked.

Remove Remote Desktop Protocol Access

To prevent unauthorized logons to the Presentation Server machine, remove Remote Desktop Protocol (RDP) access if it is not needed.

Remove RDP Access via Terminal Services Configuration

1. Click **Start > Administrative Tools > Terminal Services Configuration**.
2. In the left pane of the **Terminal Services Configuration** window, click on the **Connections** node.
3. In the right pane of the **Terminal Services Configuration** window, right click on the **RDP-tcp** connection.
4. Click **Delete**.
5. Click **Yes**.

Disable Administrative Shares

To permanently disable administrative shares on the Presentation Server machine, follow these steps:

1. Launch regedit.exe.
2. Browse to **HKEY_LOCAL_MACHINE > SYSTEM > CurrentControlSet > Services > LanManServer > Parameters**.
3. Change the value of AutoShareServer to **0**.

    If AutoShareServer does not exist, create a registry key with this name of type REG_DWORD and set its value to **0**.
4. Restart the machine.

Configure Auditing

Auditing enables the Presentation Server administrator to perform a security analysis after a system breach. Windows Server 2003 auditing is enabled in using policies. The settings shown below are recommended for a Presentation Server in the absence of any firm organizational policies on the subject. Existing organizational policies should receive preference over the settings suggested in this chapter.

To Enable Local Security Auditing in Windows Server 2003

1. Log on to the server as a Windows administrator.
2. Launch the Local Security Settings (**Start > Settings > Control Panel > Administrative Tools > Local Security Policy**).
3. Click to expand **Local Policies**.
4. Double click on **Audit Policy**. Table 7-3 shows the recommended security settings for the audit policy.
5. Exit the Local Security Settings (**File > Exit**). Reboot the Presentation Server.

Policy	Description	Security Setting
Audit account logon events	Determines whether an account logon should be recorded in the security log. The event is recorded in both the domain controller and the local security log.	Success, Failure
Audit account management	Determines whether to audit events related to users and groups. Account creation, password updates, and group membership changes all generate unique audit events.	Success, Failure
Audit directory service access	Determines whether to audit events when a user accesses an active directory object with an SACL.	No auditing
Audit logon events	Determines whether an account logon or logoff event should be generated.	Success, Failure
Audit object access	Determines whether access on objects with SACLs should generate audit events.	No auditing
Audit policy change	Determines whether changes to user rights, audit, and trust policies should generate audit events.	Success, Failure
Audit privilege use	Determines whether audit events should be generated when users exercise user rights.	Failure
Audit process tracking	Determines whether audit events for process-related events should be generated. For example, process-related events include process creation, process termination, handling duplication, and primary token assignments.	No auditing
Audit system events	Determines whether audit events should be generated when events that affect the system or security log are generated, such as computer restarts or halts.	Failure

Table 7-3.   Audit Policy Configuration

Note that the steps presented here also can be performed as part of the Local Security Policy for the Presentation Server. Refer to the section "Configure Group Policy for Presentation Server" for more information.

VERIFY THE SECURED CONFIGURATION

To verify that all the security steps have been followed, perform the following verifications. Verify that only selected ports are open and services are running:

1. Using a port scanner, scan the Presentation Server from within the DMZ.
2. Only ports configured to be open should be visible in the port scan.
3. Using the Services Control Manager, verify that only the selected services are running.

Verify that the configured authentication mechanism is working:

1. Connect to the Presentation Server with the Presentation Server Client by using the configured credentials.
2. If smart cards are used, verify that the session behaves as configured when the smart card PIN is requested and when the smart card is removed from the smart card reader.

Verify that the connection from the Presentation Server to the Presentation Server Client is encrypted:

1. Using a network monitoring tool, start a network capture.
2. From a client, log in to the Presentation Server.
3. Stop the network capture and view the results.
4. Filter the results so that only traffic between the client and the Presentation Server is displayed.
5. Confirm that all traffic between the client and the Presentation Server is encrypted.

Verify that the connection from the Presentation Server to the Web Interface is encrypted:

1. Using a network monitoring tool, start a network capture.
2. From a client, log in to the Web Interface.
3. Stop the network capture and view the results.
4. Filter the results so that only traffic between the client and the Web Interface server is displayed.
5. Confirm that all traffic between the Presentation Server and the Web Interface is encrypted.

Verify that the Presentation Server client drive mapping policy works as expected:

1. From the client, log in to the Presentation Server.
2. Attempt to navigate to one of the client drives.
3. If client drive mapping is enabled, the drive should be available; if mapping is disabled, the drive should not be visible.

Verify that the Presentation Server clipboard mapping policy works as expected:

1. From the client, log in to the Presentation Server.
2. Copy some text by pressing CTRL-C in the published application.
3. In a local client-side application, attempt to paste the text by pressing CTRL-V.
4. If clipboard mapping is enabled, the text should be copied into the client application; if it is disabled, the text should not be copied.

Verify that the Presentation Server LPT port mapping policy works as expected:

1. From the client, log in to the Presentation Server.
2. Launch an application that needs access to LPT ports.
3. If LPT port mapping is enabled, the application should be able to communicate with the client LPT ports; if it is disabled, the LPT ports should not be available.

Verify that the Presentation Server COM port mapping policy works as expected:

1. From the client, log in to the Presentation Server.
2. Launch an application that needs access to COM ports.
3. If COM port mapping is enabled, the application should be able to communicate with the client COM ports; if it is disabled, the COM ports should not be available.

Verify that the communication between the Presentation Server and the database back end is encrypted:

1. Using a network monitoring tool, start a network capture.
2. Using the Presentation Server Console, publish a new application.
3. Stop the network capture and view the results.
4. Filter the results so that only traffic between the Presentation Server and the database back end is displayed.
5. Confirm that all traffic between the Presentation Server and the database back end is encrypted.

Verify that the Citrix administrator accounts are configured as expected:

1. Launch the Presentation Server Console and log in as a Citrix administrator.

2. Attempt to perform an operation that the configured Citrix administrator is not permitted to perform.

3. Confirm that the operation is not available, or if it is attempted, confirm that it fails.

Verify that specific Citrix Connection Configuration settings are working as expected:

1. Connect to the Presentation Server with the Presentation Server Client. Confirm that only the configured client mappings are present.

2. For client drive mapping, attempt to access the client's drives.

3. For Windows client printer mapping, attempt to print a document to a client printer.

4. For client LPT port mapping, attempt to access the client LPT ports.

5. For client COM port mapping, attempt to access the client COM ports.

6. For client clipboard mapping, attempt to cut and paste text between a published application and a client-side application.

7. For client audio mapping, attempt to play back a sound using a published application.

Verify that the SNMP communication is secured:

1. Using a network monitoring tool, start a network capture.

2. Using an SNMP console, send an SNMP GET request to the Presentation Server. When the wrong community value is specified in the GET message, no response should be returned or an error will be generated.

3. Run the SNMP console on a machine that the Presentation Server SNMP service is configured to ignore SNMP messages from and send an SNMP GET query. No response should be returned.

4. Stop the network capture.

5. If IPsec was used to secure the communication, the trace should reveal only encrypted traffic.

Verify that only authorized Web Interface servers can communicate with the XML service:

1. Stop the Web Interface service.

2. Assign an IP address to the Web Interface server with which the XML Service is not configured to allow communication.

3. Restart the Web Interface service.

4. The Web Interface service should fail to start.

Verify that the configured group policies apply to the Presentation Server by logging in to the Presentation Server using the Presentation Server client.

Verify that the Microsoft Terminal Services Client cannot connect to the Presentation Server if Remote Desktop Protocol access has been removed.

Verify that administrative shares are disabled:

1. From the Presentation Server machine, navigate to **Start > Run**.

2. Enter the following text into the **Open** field:

   `\\localhost\admin$`

3. Verify that the error message returned is "**No network provider accepted the given network path**."

Verify that the Installation Manager file share is not accessible by remote desktop users who attempt to connect to the file share by using Windows Explorer.

SUMMARY

This chapter explored threats to the Citrix Presentation Server, countermeasures to each of those threats, and ways to implement each countermeasure. Always keep the operating system, antivirus software, and Citrix Presentation Server up to date with the latest security hot fixes and service packs.

CHAPTER 8

Presentation Server Client

This chapter explains how to protect the Citrix Presentation Server Client. The discussion covers the assets of the Presentation Server Client, threats to those assets, countermeasures to the threats, and instructions for implementing the countermeasures in a Presentation Server environment.

NOTE   Only version 9 of the Presentation Server Client software for the Windows XP and Windows Server 2003 32-bit platforms is discussed in this chapter.

DEPLOYMENTS

The Presentation Server Client can connect securely to a Presentation Server from an intranet via SSL Relay (Figure 8-1) or from the Internet via the Secure Gateway (Figure 8-2). This connection is known as an ICA session. Depending on an organization's network topology, the Presentation Server traffic may pass through multiple Secure Gateways (Figure 8-3). There are other connection methods for a client to connect to a Presentation Server, but these are the most common ones. For a more detailed discussion of the authentication and secure communication mechanisms that can protect an ICA session, refer to Chapter 2, "Secure Deployments."

If the session reliability feature is enabled, the traffic from the Secure Gateway to the Presentation Server will be over the session reliability port, 2598. Connections using SSL Relay will communicate over port 443 by default regardless of whether session reliability is enabled.

COMPONENTS

The Presentation Server Client package contains the Win32 client-side component of the Citrix Presentation Server. The client is used to connect to a Presentation Server and access published resources. Published resources include applications and documents that are published on a Presentation Server. Running the latest version of the Presentation Server Client software is encouraged. Check http://www.citrix.com periodically for an updated version of the Presentation Server Client.

Pass-Through Client

The Pass-Through Client is a form of the Presentation Server Client that allows it to be used as a published application. Its behavior is slightly different from that of the Presentation Server Client that is run from workstations and laptops. Presentation Server users launch the Pass-Through Client as a published application. The Pass-Through Client in turn connects to a second Presentation Server and runs either another published application or desktop. The Pass-Through Client therefore relays the ICA session from the second Presentation Server to the client on the user's client machine.

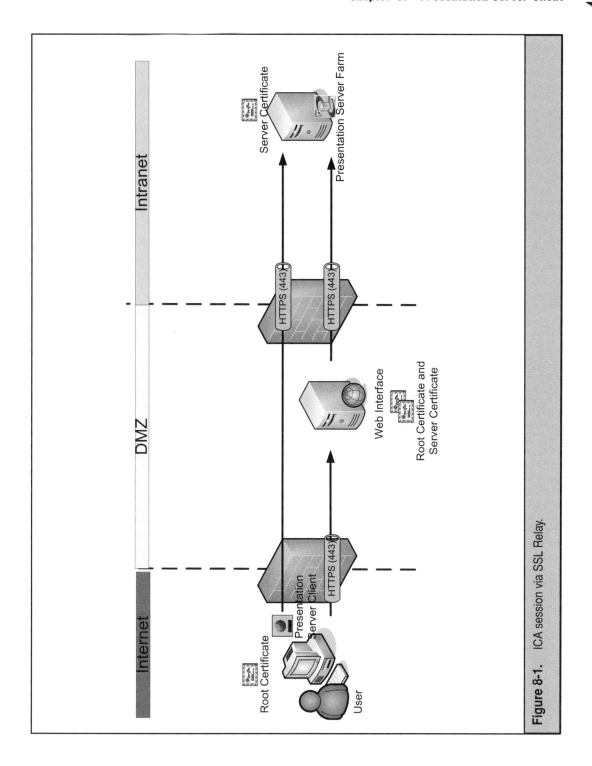

Figure 8-1. ICA session via SSL Relay.

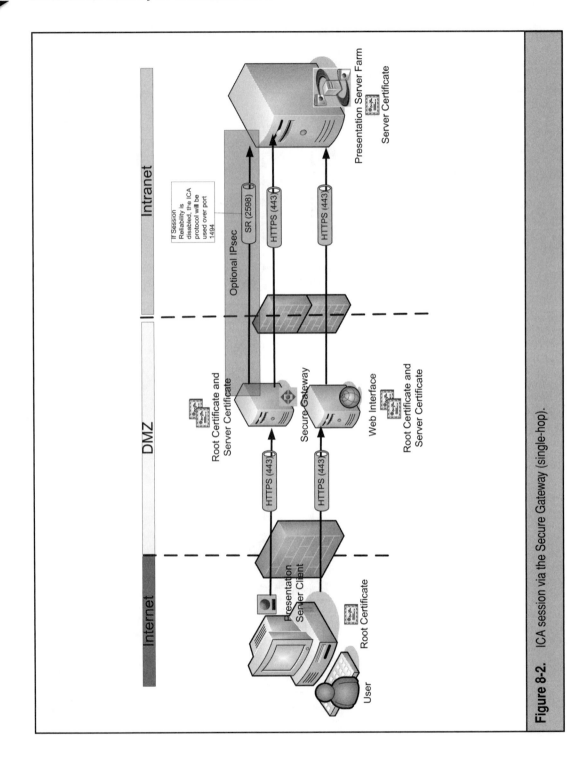

Figure 8-2. ICA session via the Secure Gateway (single-hop).

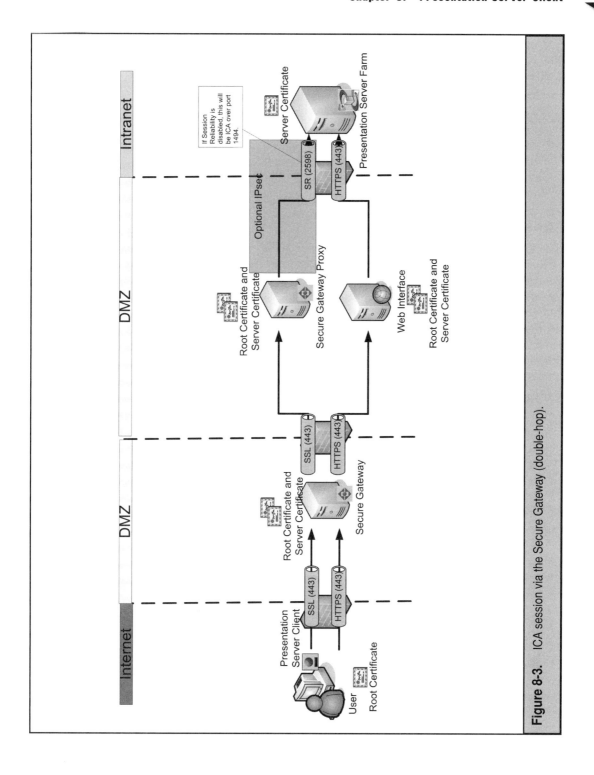

Figure 8-3.   ICA session via the Secure Gateway (double-hop).

NOTE   Pass-through authentication, as described later in this chapter, is not related to the Pass-Through Client.

Program Neighborhood

The Program Neighborhood Client is configured and managed by each individual user. Program Neighborhood cannot be configured from a centralized site such as the Program Neighborhood Agent site; thus, it does not require a Web Interface for the Presentation Server.

Program Neighborhood Agent

The Program Neighborhood Agent is a client that supports the full Presentation Server feature set. A subset of the Program Neighborhood Agent functionality is centrally administered and configured in the Citrix Access Suite Console, using a Web Interface Program Neighborhood Agent site. Security settings can be dictated by the Web Interface, but client security settings always take precedence. The Program Neighborhood Agent works in the background. Except for a shortcut menu available from the Windows notification area, it does not have a user interface. Data transfer from the client to the Web Interface occurs over the HTTP or HTTPS protocols.

Web Client

The Web Client is a smaller client that allows for quick distribution. It is available in .cab file format for Internet Explorer users for quick downloading and installation. Users access published resources from within their Web browsers by clicking links on a corporate intranet or Internet Web page accessed via HTTP or HTTPS. Clicking a link launches the published resource within the same browser window or in a new, separate browser window.

ASSETS

The assets of the Presentation Server Client include the following:

▼ *Bitmap disk cache.* The security characteristics of this asset are confidentiality and integrity.

■ *Configuration data.* The security characteristics of this asset are confidentiality and integrity.

■ *ICA browsing session data.* The security characteristics of this asset are confidentiality and integrity.

■ *ICA session data.* The security characteristics of this asset are confidentiality and integrity.

- ■ *Password.* The security characteristic of this asset is confidentiality.
- ▲ *Web Interface session data.* The security characteristics of this asset are confidentiality and integrity.

The assets of the client machine include the following:

- ▼ *Client devices.* The security characteristics of this asset are confidentiality, integrity, and availability.
- ■ *Clipboard data.* The security characteristics of this asset are confidentiality and integrity.
- ▲ *Files stored on the client machine.* The security characteristics of this asset are confidentiality and integrity.

THREATS AND COUNTERMEASURES

The most common threats to the Presentation Server Client are

- ▼ Disclosure of the password
- ■ Disclosure of ICA session data
- ■ Disclosure of client files
- ■ Malicious servers
- ■ Unauthorized access to client devices
- ■ Tampering with client files
- ▲ Tampering with client configuration

Disclosure of Password

The password used by the Presentation Server Client to authenticate to a Presentation Server must be protected when it is sent across the network to a server.

If the client connects to a malicious server, the password can be disclosed to it. The password also may be disclosed to an unintended third party who has access to the network if the ICA session data are not encrypted.

Countermeasures

The countermeasures to threat of password disclosure while it is in transit to the Presentation Server include the following:

- ▼ Use Kerberos authentication. The password will not be sent across the network.
- ■ Use strong authentication, such as a smart card, to remove the risk of password disclosure.
- ▲ Use SSL/TLS to protect the confidentiality of the password.

Disclosure of ICA Session Data

The data transmitted during an ICA session may contain screen display or keystrokes that describe confidential information. This network traffic may be observed by an attacker if it is sent across a network unencrypted. Also, session graphic data may be eavesdropped upon if they are cached in the Presentation Server's bitmap disk cache.

Countermeasures

The countermeasures to this threat consist of the following:

▼ Protect the confidentiality of data communicated between the Presentation Server Client and Presentation Servers with SSL/TLS.

▲ Prevent screen updates from being stored in the bitmap disk cache.

Disclosure of Client Files

Files stored on the client machine may be vulnerable to disclosure when at rest on the client machine, as well as in transit, when they are sent across the network to a server.

Countermeasures

The countermeasures to this threat in the Presentation Server Client include the following:

▼ Use SSL/TLS for all network communication to protect the confidentiality of the files.

■ Disable client drive mapping if it is not needed.

▲ Disable clipboard mapping if it is not needed.

Malicious Servers

Without authentication of the server, the wrong server could be connected to. A user could be lured into connecting to a malicious server. The server spoofing threat introduces risks of password disclosure and unauthorized access to client files, documents, and devices.

Countermeasures

The countermeasures to this threat are as follows:

▼ Authenticate server identity. A server's identity will be authenticated by the Presentation Server Client when SSL/TLS connections are used.

▲ Enable certificate revocation list checking.

Unauthorized Access to Client Devices

Devices that are connected to the client computer may be vulnerable to tampering or information disclosure attacks if the client connects to an untrusted server. Unauthorized access to image capture devices or microphones could pose a threat to confidentiality and privacy. If the devices do not need to be accessed in an ICA session, ICA session access to them can be disabled. These client devices are

▼ Printers

■ Serial and parallel ports

■ Scanners, digital cameras, and webcams

■ Personal digital assistants

▲ Microphones

Countermeasures

The countermeasures to this threat in the Presentation Server Client include the following:

▼ Use SSL/TLS for all network communication to authenticate the server connections.

▲ Disable client device mapping for client devices that do not need to be accessed via the ICA connection.

Tampering with Client Files

Files stored on the client may be vulnerable to tampering via the ICA session when at rest on the client machine, as well as in transit, when they are sent across the network to a server. All files on the client machine may be at risk if the client is run by an administrator.

Countermeasures

The countermeasures to this threat in the Presentation Server Client include the following:

▼ Use SSL/TLS to protect the integrity of all network communication.

■ Disable client drive mapping if it is not needed.

■ Disable clipboard mapping if it is not needed.

▲ Run the client only as a nonprivileged user.

Tampering with Client Configuration

Client configuration data stored on the client may be vulnerable to tampering.

Countermeasures

The countermeasures to this threat include the following:

▼ Maintain proper access controls on client configuration data.

■ Run the client as only a nonprivileged user.

▲ Use New Technology File System (NTFS) partitions.

STEPS FOR SECURING PRESENTATION SERVER CLIENT

The following steps for securing the Presentation Server Client are discussed below:

- ▼ Configure authentication.
- ■ Configure secure communications.
- ■ Run the client only as a nonprivileged user.
- ■ Disable client drive mapping.
- ■ Disable undesired device mappings.
- ▲ Disable the bitmap disk cache.

Configure Authentication

Kerberos Pass-Through Authentication

Rather than sending user passwords over the network, pass-through authentication can be performed by using Kerberos authentication. Kerberos is an industry-standard network authentication protocol that is built into Microsoft Windows operating systems. The Presentation Server Clients can be configured to use the Windows Kerberos Security Service Provider to authenticate to a Presentation Server.

TIP   Use Kerberos authentication for all Presentation Server Clients that connect from the intranet or VPN.

Kerberos logon offers security-minded users or administrators the convenience of pass-through authentication combined with secret-key cryptography and data integrity provided by industry-standard network security solutions. With Kerberos logon, the ICA client does not need to handle the user's password, preventing Trojan horse–style attacks on the client machine to gain access to users' passwords.

Users can log on to the client machine with any authentication method, for example, a biometric authenticator such as a fingerprint reader, and access published resources by using Kerberos authentication without further prompts for credentials.

System Requirements   Kerberos logon requires Presentation Server 3.0 or later. Kerberos works only between clients and servers that belong to the same trusted Windows 2000 or Windows 2003 domains. Servers also must be *trusted for delegation*, an option configured through the Active Directory Users and Computers management tool.

Kerberos logon is not available in the following circumstances:

▼ Connections configured with any of the following options in Terminal Services Configuration on the server:

   ■ On the **General** tab, use the **Use standard Windows authentication** option.

   ■ On the **Logon Settings** tab, use the **Always use the following logon information** option or the **Always prompt for password** option.

■ Connections routed through the Secure Gateway for the Presentation Server.

■ If the server running the Presentation Server requires smart card logon.

▲ If the authenticated user account requires a smart card for interactive logon.

Configure Kerberos Authentication   The client, by default, is not configured to use Kerberos authentication when logging on to the server. The client can be configured to use Kerberos with or without pass-through authentication. Restricting the client to Kerberos without pass-through authentication is more secure than using Kerberos with pass-through authentication and is the recommended setting for Presentation Server Clients who are connecting from an intranet where Kerberos is always supported by the servers.

Restrict the Client to Kerberos Authentication Only   With this configuration, the user needs to authenticate only to the client machine. When the user connects to a Presentation Server, the client will use the Windows Kerberos Security Service Provider to authenticate to the Presentation Server for the user. The user will not have to reenter her or his credentials to connect to the Presentation Server. If Kerberos logon fails for any reason, the user is prompted for her or his Presentation Server credentials. The Presentation Server Client will not attempt to send a cached copy of the user's password to the Presentation Server if Kerberos authentication fails. Kerberos can fail as a result of a missing operating system requirement, such as the requirement that the server be trusted for delegation. This is the recommended setting for Presentation Server Clients who are connecting from an intranet where Kerberos is always supported by the servers.

To configure the Wfclient.ini file on the client device for Kerberos logon, do the following:

1. Log on to the client device as an administrator.

2. Launch Program Neighborhood.

3. Click **Tools > ICA Settings**.

4. In the **General** tab of the **ICA Settings** window, ensure that the **Pass-Through Authentication** setting is checked.

5. Close Program Neighborhood.

6. Open Wfclient.ini from the `C:\Program Files\Citrix\ICA Client` directory in a text editor and ensure that Wfclient.ini has the following settings:

   `SSPIEnabled=on`

```
UseSSPIOnly=on
```

7. Log off from the client device.

8. For each user,

   ▼ Log on to the client device.

   ■ Launch Program Neighborhood.

   ■ Click **ICA Settings**.

   ■ In the **General** tab of the **ICA Settings** window, ensure that the **Use local credentials to log on** setting is checked.

   ■ Click **OK**.

   ■ For each ICA connection,

      ■ Right click on the ICA connection and click **Properties**.

      ■ In the **Logon Information** tab, ensure that **Local user** is selected and **Pass-through authentication** is checked.

      ■ Click **OK**.

   ▲ Close Program Neighborhood.

Kerberos with Password Pass-Through Authentication   When client configurations are set to use Kerberos with password pass-through authentication, the client attempts to use Kerberos authentication first. Kerberos with pass-through authentication falls back to password pass-through authentication if Kerberos authentication fails. With password pass-through authentication, the Presentation Server Client sends a cached copy of the user's password to the Presentation Server. This means that the password can end up being sent over the network during authentication if Kerberos is not available. Therefore, it is recommended that **Kerberos Pass-Through Authentication Only** be used instead. Use Kerberos with Password Pass-Through Authentication only when pass-through authentication to servers that do not support Kerberos, such as Presentation Server for UNIX, is necessary.

CAUTION This configuration is less secure than using Kerberos without pass-through authentication.

To configure the Wfclient.ini file on the client device for Kerberos with password pass-through authentication, do the following:

1. Log on to the client device as an administrator.

2. Launch Program Neighborhood.

3. Click **Tools > ICA Settings**.

4. In the **General** tab of the **ICA Settings** window, ensure that the **Pass-Through Authentication** setting is checked.

5. Close Program Neighborhood.

6. Open Wfclient.ini from the C:\Program Files\Citrix\ICA Client directory in a text editor and ensure that Wfclient.ini has the following settings:

   SSPIEnabled=on

   UseSSPIOnly=off

7. Log off from the client device.

8. For each user,

   ▼ Log on to the client device.

   ■ Launch Program Neighborhood.

   ■ Click **ICA Settings**.

   ■ In the **General** tab of the **ICA Settings** window, ensure that the **Use local credentials to log on** setting is checked.

   ■ Click **OK**.

   ■ For each ICA connection,

      ■ Right click on the ICA connection and click **Properties**.

      ■ In the **Logon Information** tab, ensure that **Local user** is selected and **Pass-through authentication** is checked.

      ■ Click **OK**.

   ▲ Close Program Neighborhood.

Smart Card Authentication

This section assumes that smart card support is enabled on the server that is running the Presentation Server and that the client machine is configured with third-party smart card hardware and software. Refer to the documentation that came with the smart card equipment for instructions about deploying smart cards.

The smart card removal policy set on the Presentation Server determines what happens on the server if the smart card is removed from the reader during an ICA session. The smart card removal policy is configured through and handled by the Windows operating system. For more information on Presentation Server smart card settings, see Chapter 7, "Presentation Server."

Smart Card Logon with Pass-Through Authentication   Pass-through authentication requires that a smart card be inserted in the smart card reader at logon time only. With this logon mode selected, the client prompts the user for a smart card PIN (personal identification number) at start-up. Pass-through authentication then caches the PIN and passes it to the server every time the user requests a published resource. The user does not have to reenter a PIN to access published resources or have the smart card inserted continuously.

If authentication based on the cached PIN fails or if a published resource itself requires user authentication, the user continues to be prompted for a PIN. For more information about pass-through authentication, see the section "Kerberos Pass-Through Authentication."

Smart Card Logon Without Pass-Through Authentication Disabling pass-through authentication requires that a smart card be present in the smart card reader whenever the user accesses a server. With pass-through disabled, the client prompts the user for a smart card PIN at start-up and every time the user requests a published resource.

Configure Secure Communications

Communication between the client and the Presentation Server is secured by SSL/TLS. For more information on secure communications and how they work, see Chapter 2, "Secure Deployments."

Enable SSL and TLS

SSL and TLS are configured in the same way, use the same certificates, and are enabled simultaneously. When SSL and TLS are enabled, each time a connection is initiated, the client tries to use TLS first and then falls back to SSL. If the client cannot connect with SSL, the connection fails and an error message appears.

Install a Root Certificate on Client

To use SSL/TLS to secure communications between SSL/TLS-enabled clients and the server farm, a root certificate must be present on the client machine that can verify the signature of the Certificate Authority on the server certificate.

The clients support the Certificate Authorities that are supported by the Windows operating system. The root certificates for these Certificate Authorities are installed with Windows and managed by using Windows utilities. They are the same root certificates that are used by Microsoft Internet Explorer.

If an organization's own Certificate Authority is used, a root certificate from that Certificate Authority must be obtained and installed on each client machine. That root certificate then is used and trusted by both Microsoft Internet Explorer and the client.

Depending on the organization's policies and procedures, the root certificate can be distributed to each client machine instead of directing users to install it. Root certificates can be distributed and installed by using Windows 2003 Group Policy to clients that operate in an active directory environment. See the Microsoft Windows 2003 documentation for more information.

Alternatively, root certificates can be installed by using other administration or deployment methods, such as the following:

▼   Microsoft Internet Explorer Administration Kit (IEAK) Configuration Wizard and Profile Manager

■   Microsoft Active Directory Group Policy

▲   Third-party deployment tools

Make sure that the certificates installed by the Windows operating system meet the organization's security requirements or use the certificates issued by the organization's Certificate Authority.

Use SSL/TLS+HTTPS for ICA Browsing

With SSL/TLS+HTTPS as the network protocol, the client uses the HTTPS protocol to search for a list of servers that are running the Presentation Server. The client communicates with the server by using ICA with SSL/TLS. SSL/TLS+HTTPS provides strong encryption of ICA traffic and server authentication.

If SSL/TLS+HTTPS is selected as the network protocol, the fully qualified domain name of the server that is hosting the digital certificate must be entered into the **Server** address field in the client's user interface.

NOTE   The SSL/TLS+HTTPS protocols can be used only with compatible servers running the Presentation Server. See the *Presentation Server Administrator's Guide* for Windows or UNIX for information about configuring the server running the Presentation Server to use SSL/TLS.

To Configure Program Neighborhood to Use SSL/TLS

1.   Open Program Neighborhood.

2.   To configure an application set to use SSL/TLS:

Right click the application set to be configured and select **Application Set Settings**. A **Settings** dialog box for the application set appears.

To configure an existing custom ICA connection to use SSL/TLS:

Right click the custom ICA connection to be configured and select **Properties**. The **Properties** dialog box for the custom connection appears.

To configure all future custom ICA connections to use SSL/TLS:

Right click in a blank area of the **Custom ICA Connections** window and select **Custom Connections Settings**. The **Custom ICA Connections** dialog box appears.

3.   To configure an application set or an existing custom ICA connection:

From the **Network Protocol** menu, select **SSL/TLS+HTTPS**.

To configure all future custom ICA connections:

From the **Network Protocol** menu, select **HTTP/HTTPS**.

4. Add the fully qualified domain name of the SSL/TLS-enabled servers running the Presentation Server to the Address List.

5. Click **OK.**

To Configure Program Neighborhood Agent to Use SSL/TLS

To use secure HTTP (HTTPS) to encrypt the configuration information passed between the Program Neighborhood Agent and the server that is running the Web Interface, enter the server URL in the format https://<servername> on the **Server** tab of the Program Neighborhood Agent **Properties** dialog box.

Enable Certificate Revocation List Checking

When certificate revocation list checking is enabled, the clients check whether the server's certificate is revoked. Clients must check this.

Different certificate revocation list checking behaviors can be configured. For example, the client can be configured to check only its local certificate list or to check the local and network certificate lists. In addition, certificate checking can be configured to allow users to log on only if all certificate revocation lists are verified.

To Enable Certificate Revocation List Checking

1. With a text editor, open the appsrv.ini file in each user's Documents and Settings\Application Data\ICA Client directory

2. In the [WFClient] section of appsrv.ini, set the **SSLCertificateRevocationCheckPolicy** value to one of the values described in Table 8-1.

Value	Meaning	Check Local CRL Stores	Check CRL Distribution Points	Pass or Fail Certificate Verification if No CRL Is Found
NoCheck	No certificate revocation list checking is performed. Use this option if no CRL checking is desired.	No	No	Pass

Table 8-1. Certificate Revocation List Settings

Value	Meaning	Check Local CRL Stores	Check CRL Distribution Points	Pass or Fail Certificate Verification if No CRL Is Found
CheckWith NoNetwork Access	Any CRLs that have been previously installed or downloaded will be used in certificate validation. If a certificate is found to have been revoked, the connection will fail. Use this option if certificate revocation lists are distributed offline.	Yes	No	Pass
FullAccess Check	The client will attempt to retrieve CRLs from the relevant certificate issuers. If a certificate is found to have been revoked, the connection will fail. Use this option if CRLs are distributed via the network.	Yes	Yes	Pass
FullAccess CheckAnd CRL Required	The client will attempt to retrieve CRLs from the distribution point specified by the certificate issuer in the certificate. If a certificate is found to have been revoked, the connection will fail. If the client is unable to retrieve a valid CRL, the connection will fail. Use this option for mandatory CRL checking.	Yes	Yes	Fail

Table 8-1.   Certificate Revocation List Settings (continued)

NOTE   The default setting is CheckWithNoNetworkAccess.

3. Save the changes to appsrv.ini.

Run the Client Only as a Nonprivileged User

To minimize the impact of an attack on the Presentation Server Client, do not run any Presentation Server Client software as a privileged user. Privileged users include administrators, power users, and any other users who have been granted special privileges or permissions. Instead, run the client under a regular user account that is not in the administrators group. This will limit the impact to the client system if the ICA session is attacked.

Disable Client Drive Mapping

When client drive mapping is disabled, the client will completely deny client drive mapping access to the client's file system. This stops the DLL that is implementing the client drive mapping virtual channel (vdcdm30n.dll) from loading on client start-up.

1. With a text editor, open the module.ini file from the Citrix\ICA Client directory.

2. In the **[ICA 3.0]** section of module.ini, remove **ClientDrive** from the list of virtual drivers in the **VirtualDriver** value. This will prevent the client drive mapping support from being loaded by the Presentation Server Client.

3. Save the changes to module.ini.

Disable Undesired Device Mappings

To minimize the attack surface of the ICA connection, disable any unneeded device mappings. For example, if client printer mapping is not permitted by security policy and will never be used, the client printer mapping virtual channel can be disabled. These client devices are

▼ Printers and parallel ports

■ Serial ports

■ Scanners, digital cameras, and webcams

■ Personal digital assistants

▲ Microphones

Disable Client Printer and Parallel Port Mapping

When client printer and port mapping are disabled, the client prevents the server from accessing or printing to printers available to the client machine.

1. With a text editor, open the module.ini file from the Citrix\ICA Client directory.

2. In the **[ICA 3.0]** section of module.ini, remove **ClientPrinterQueue** and **ClientPrinterPort** from the list of virtual drivers in the **VirtualDriver** value. This will prevent the client printer and parallel port mapping support from being loaded by the Presentation Server Client.

3. Save the changes to module.ini.

Disable Personal Digital Assistant Mapping

To disable server access to personal digital assistants connected to the client machine, follow the steps for disabling serial port mapping.

Disable Serial Port Mapping

When serial port mapping is disabled, the client prevents the server from accessing serial ports and personal digital assistant devices available to the client machine.

NOTE   Disabling serial port mapping will also disable personal digital assistant synchronization.

1. With a text editor, open the module.ini file from the Citrix\ICA Client directory.

2. In the **[ICA 3.0]** section of module.ini, remove **ClientComm** from the list of virtual drivers in the **VirtualDriver** value. This will prevent the client serial port mapping support from being loaded by the Presentation Server Client.

3. Save the changes to module.ini.

Disable Image Capture Mapping

When image capture mapping is disabled, the client prevents the server from accessing image capture devices available to the client machine, such as scanners, digital cameras, and webcams.

1. With a text editor, open the module.ini file from the Citrix\ICA Client directory.

2. In the **[ICA 3.0]** section of module.ini, remove **TwainRdr** from the list of virtual drivers in the **VirtualDriver** value. This will prevent the client image capture mapping support from being loaded by the Presentation Server Client.

3. Save the changes to module.ini.

Disable Client Microphone Mapping

When client microphone mapping is disabled, the client prevents the server from accessing microphones available to the client machine.

1. With a text editor, open the module.ini file from the Citrix\ICA Client directory.

2. In the **[ICA 3.0]** section of module.ini, remove **ClientAudio** and **SpeechMike** from the list of virtual drivers in the **VirtualDriver** value. This will prevent the client microphone and SpeechMike mapping support from being loaded by the Presentation Server Client.

3. Save the changes to module.ini.

Disable Clipboard Mapping

When clipboard mapping is disabled, the client prevents the server from copying or pasting from the clipboard available to the client machine. No clipboard data will be sent from the client to the server or from the server to the client. Disabling clipboard mapping will not affect use of the server clipboard on the server or use of the client clipboard on the client.

1. With a text editor, open the module.ini file from the Citrix\ICA Client directory.

2. In the **[ICA 3.0]** section of module.ini, remove **Clipboard** from the list of virtual drivers in the **VirtualDriver** value. This will prevent the client clipboard mapping support from being loaded by the Presentation Server Client.

3. Save the changes to module.ini.

Disable Bitmap Disk Cache

If the Presentation Server Client will be connecting over a high-speed connection, such as a local area network (LAN), bitmap caching is not necessary. On slower connections such as wide area networks (WANs) and dial-up, the bitmap caching will improve the performance of the ICA connection. The bitmap cache is protected by an ACL so that only the user can view its contents, but the cache will still be stored to disk, and so there could still be a threat to the confidentiality of the data. The bitmap caching should be disabled if it is not needed to improve the performance of the ICA connection.

1. With a text editor, open the appsrv.ini file in each user's Documents and Settings\Application Data\ICA Client directory.

2. In the **[WFClient]** section of appsrv.ini, set the following value:

   ```
   PersistentCacheEnabled=off
   ```

3. Save the changes to appsrv.ini.

VERIFY THE SECURED CONFIGURATION

To verify that all the security steps have been followed, do the following:

1. From a different machine, run a port scanner and verify that only the expected ports are open.

2. Connect to a Presentation Server. Try to access disabled devices such as mapped printers or drives. The access should fail.

3. Connect to a Presentation Server with a revoked server certificate. The connection should fail depending on the CRL setting.

4. From a different machine on the same network, run a packet sniffer. Connect to a Presentation Server. Verify that the password used to authenticate to the server is not viewable from the packet sniffer.

5. From a different machine on the same network, run a packet analyzer. Connect to a Presentation Server. Verify that the packets sent in the connection to the server are using the SSL/TLS protocol.

SUMMARY

This chapter has explored threats to the Citrix Presentation Server Client, countermeasures to each of those threats, and ways to implement each countermeasure. Always keep the operating system and antivirus software up to date with the latest security hot fixes and service packs and check the Citrix website regularly for the latest version of the Citrix Presentation Server Client.

CHAPTER 9

License Server

This chapter explains how to protect the Citrix License Server. The discussion covers the assets of License Server, threats to those assets, countermeasures to the threats, and instructions for implementing the countermeasures in a Citrix environment. Every Access Suite deployment must have at least one shared or dedicated license server. Before running, Access Suite products must obtain a license from the license server. License servers store and manage Citrix licenses, allowing the licenses to be shared across the network for different Citrix products. To track licenses, license servers store and use license files. To manage the license server, Citrix provides the License Management Console.

DEPLOYMENTS

Citrix Licensing is designed to centrally manage and distribute purchased licenses to deployed Citrix products.

COMPONENTS

Citrix License Server

The service that allows administrators to centrally manage licenses and lets clients utilize those licenses is known as the Citrix License Server.

License Files

License files are files that allow Citrix products to function. These files are stored on the license server and contain the following information:

▼ The license server name

■ The Citrix Licensing service port number

■ The Subscription Advantage Membership renewal date

▲ The license expiration date (early adopter, technical preview, and developer edition licenses only)

License Management Console

The License Management Console is the Web-based management interface for the Citrix License Server. This optional interface runs on Apache Tomcat and provides remote administration and monitoring of a license server.

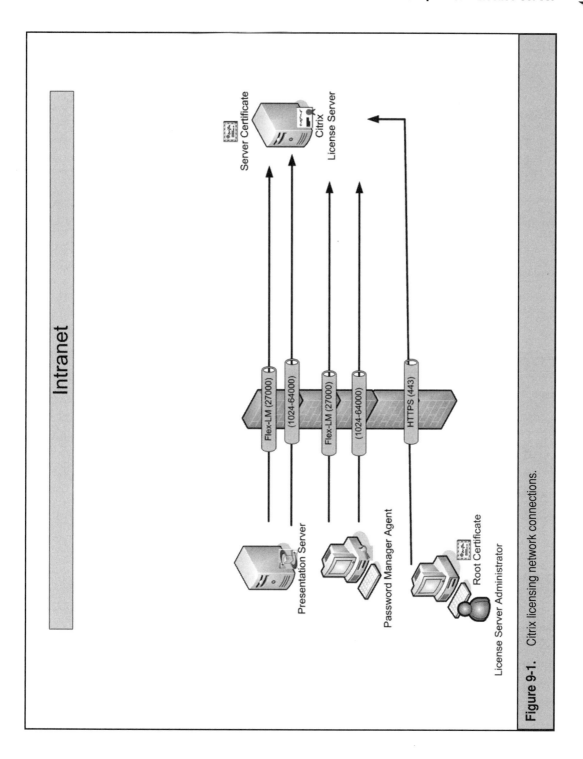

Figure 9-1. Citrix licensing network connections.

License Administration Commands

The License Management Console provides a method of accessing many administrative licensing features. Alternatively, administrators can perform licensing tasks by using license administration commands. Situations in which administrators might want to use license administration commands include the following:

▼   When the administrator did not install the License Management Console

▲   When the administrator is performing advanced operations on the license server that are not available in the License Management Console

These commands allow administration of the license server without the License Management Console or remote access to the license server, thus reducing the server's attack surface.

License Server Options File

The license server options file defines licensing behavior—the number of licenses a product server can use—and the location of the license server logs.

ASSETS

The license server has the following assets:

▼   *License server service.* The security characteristics of this asset are availability and auditability.

■   *Log files.* The security characteristics of this asset are confidentiality and integrity.

■   *License files.* The security characteristics of this asset are confidentiality, integrity, and availability.

▲   *License options file.* The security characteristics of this asset are confidentiality and integrity.

THREATS AND COUNTERMEASURES

The license server may be targeted by an attacker. If the license server is unavailable, Citrix Access Suite products cannot obtain Citrix licenses. The main threats to a license server are

▼   Service disruption

■   Unauthorized access to the license server service

▲   Worms, viruses, and other malicious software

Service Disruption

Service disruptions can be caused by system failure, human error, or malicious behavior. System failures include hardware failure and power failure. Human errors include accidental deletion of files. Malicious behavior consists of denial-of-service attacks.

Countermeasures

Countermeasures to nonmalicious service disruptions include the following:

▼ Restrict access to the Citrix License Server.

■ Restrict the permissions of those who have access.

▲ Use backups.

Countermeasures to denial-of-service attacks include log files.

These countermeasures are useful because restricting access to license server functions limits the damage that any single person can do. Backups allow for recovery from service disruptions and malicious software. Audit trails provide a mechanism for identifying attackers.

Unauthorized Access to the License Server Service

Unauthorized access to the license server service occurs when a user executes restricted license server functions that organizational policies do not authorize that user to execute. Attackers can gain unauthorized access to license server services in two ways:

▼ Physically reaching the machine

▲ Remotely connecting to the server

If an attacker physically accesses the license server, he or she can do a variety of malicious things, such as the following:

▼ Restart the machine and use various tools to circumvent operating system security

▲ Log in at the console

If someone has remote access to the license server, that person can

▼ Attempt to check out all the licenses

■ Launch network-based attacks against the operating system and services running on the server

■ Launch a denial-of-service attack against the server

▲ View the log files

Countermeasures

Preventing unauthorized access to the license server service means ensuring that only those who need access to the license server can get it. It is important to ensure that different individuals have different roles. The individuals responsible for maintaining the hardware of the license server may not need to configure users on the license server. License server administrators do not need to be Windows administrators and do not require physical access to the machine.

Countermeasures to unauthorized access of the license server service include the following:

▼ Restrict who can reach (physically and remotely) the license server.

■ Set appropriate ACLs on configuration and log files.

■ Grant individuals only the permissions within the License Management Console that they require to fulfill their roles.

▲ Use SSL/TLS for administrative network communication to and from the server.

These countermeasures help limit the number of users who can do damage and the amount of damage any single user can do.

Worms, Viruses, and Other Malicious Software

Software that performs automated malicious operations on the server can disrupt the availability of the license server's services.

Countermeasures

The most effective countermeasures against malicious software include the following:

▼ Protective network-based hardware

■ Protective network-based software

■ Protective host-based software

▲ Limit the exposure of the server

Protective network-based hardware such as a firewall helps prevent unauthorized communication with the server. Software such as intrusion prevention systems attempts to prevent attack traffic from reaching hosts. Intrusion detection systems monitor for suspicious activity. These systems can be network-based, host-based, or both. Similarly, host-based software such as antivirus software and antispyware software helps prevent malicious software from damaging the server. To limit the exposure of the server, do not run client software such as Web browsers or instant messaging clients on the server.

Whenever possible, it is advisable to use a dedicated license server. A dedicated license server offers several security benefits over a license server that runs on the same machine as other Citrix products. Dedicated license servers have a smaller attack surface since they are running fewer applications, and they can be protected more tightly by firewalls and access restrictions for the same reason. Additionally, if a dedicated server is compromised or fails, other servers may not be affected.

STEPS FOR SECURING THE CITRIX LICENSE SERVER

The following steps for securing the Citrix License Server are discussed below:

▼ Secure the operating system.

■ Download the license files.

■ Protect the license files.

■ Protect the log files.

■ Restrict access to the License Management Console.

■ Isolate the Citrix License Server behind a firewall.

▲ Configure auditing.

Secure the Operating System

The Windows 2003 Security Configuration Wizard allows administrators to secure the operating system. It provides a mechanism to lock down the ports used by various services and disable Windows services that are unnecessary. The options that appear while one is running the Windows Server 2003 Security Configuration Wizard vary with the choices made along the way.

NOTE   Administrators may have to modify these steps to account for installed applications such as antivirus or firewall software.

To install and run the Security Configuration Wizard, do the following:

1. Log on to the server as a Windows administrator.

2. Launch the Add or Remove Programs tool (**Start > Control Panel > Add or Remove Programs**).

3. Click **Add/Remove Windows Components** to bring up the **Windows Components Wizard**.

4. Select the **Security Configuration Wizard** check box and click **Next**. A number of progress messages temporarily appear.

5. When the installation is complete, click **Finish**.

6. Close the **Add or Remove Programs** dialog box.

7. Launch the Security Configuration Wizard (**Start > Administrative Tools > Security Configuration Wizard**).

8. At the **Welcome** screen, click **Next**.

9. At the **Configuration Action** screen, ensure that **Create a new security policy** is selected and click **Next**.

10. At the **Select Server** screen, leave the default value and click **Next**.

11. At the **Processing Security Configuration Database** screen, wait for the system scan to complete and click **Next**.

12. At the **Role-Based Service Configuration** screen, click **Next**.

13. A **Select Server Roles** screen appears. The options that administrators should select from this screen and all subsequent screens vary with the machine to which they are applying the Security Configuration Wizard. Each of the subsequent screens requires the selection of the different options listed in Table 9-1.

Screen	Options
Select Server Roles	Web server
Select Client Features	DNS client
	Domain member
	Microsoft networking client
Select Administration and Other Options	Time synchronization
	Windows firewall
Select Additional Services	Citrix Licensing WMI
	Citrix Licensing
	License Management Console for Citrix Licensing (optional)
Handling Unspecified Services	Do not change the start-up mode of the service. Confirm Service
Changes	Click **Next**.
Network Security	Leave **Skip this section** cleared and click **Next**.
Open Ports and Approved Applications	123 (NTP)
	443 (HTTPS)
	Ports used by Citrix Licensing WMI (Citrix_GTLicensingProv.exe)
	Ports used by CitrixLicensing (lmgrd.exe)
	Ports used by Citrix License Management Console (tomcat.exe)
	Ports used by Citrix.exe. To do this, click **Add**, select the **Approve Application** tab, type C:\ ProgramFiles\Citrix\Licensing\LS\CITRIX.exe, and click **OK**.

Table 9-1. Security Configuration Wizard

Screen	Options
Confirm Port Configuration	Click **Next**.
Registry Settings	Leave **Skip this section** cleared and click **Next**.
Require SMB Security Signatures	Leave **All computers that connect to it satisfy the minimum operating system requirements** checked.
	Leave **It has surplus process capacity that can be used to sign the file and print traffic** checked.
	Click **Next**.
Outbound Authentication Methods	Domain accounts
Outbound Authentication Using Domain Accounts	Windows NT 4.0 Service Pack 6a or later operating systems
Inbound Authentication Methods	N/A
Registry Settings Summary	Click **Next**.
Audit Policy	Leave the **Skip this section** check box cleared and click **Next**.
	Select **Audit successful and unsuccessful activities**.
	Click **Next**.
Internet Information Services	Leave **Skip this section** cleared and click **Next**.
Select Web Service Extensions for Dynamic Content	Tomcat Servlet Engine Prohibit all other Web service extensions not listed above.
Select the Virtual Directories to Retain	None
Prevent Anonymous Users from Accessing Content Files	Deny anonymous users Write access to content files.
IIS Settings Summary	Click **Next**.

Table 9-1. Security Configuration Wizard (continued)

14. At the **Save Security Policy** screen, click **Next**.

15. At the **Security Policy File Name** screen, type an appropriate name in the **Security policy file name** box and click **Next**.

16. In the dialog box that appears suggesting that a server restart is required, click **OK**.

17. At the **Apply Security Policy** screen, select **Apply Now** and click **Next**. An **Applying Security Policy** screen appears while the security policy is applied.

18. At the **Applying Security Policy** screen, click **Next**.

19. At the **Completing the Security Configuration Wizard** screen, click **Finish**.

20. Restart the server for the security policies to take effect.

NOTE After completing these steps, administrators will still have to follow their regular procedures for securing a server.

Download License Files

To download license files from the MyCitrix web site, administrators will need

▼ A computer connected to the Internet

■ Portable storage for the license files (CD-R is recommended)

■ The customized product license code that was sent by e-mail (Citrix License Authorization Code—Order ID)

■ The hostname of the license server

▲ The number of licenses to allocate

To download license files, follow these steps:

1. Launch Internet Explorer (**Start > All Programs > Internet Explorer**), and in Internet Explorer's **Address** bar type http://www.MyCitrix.com and press **Enter**.

2. At the **MyCitrix Login** page, enter the appropriate credentials in the **Login ID** box and in the **Password** box and click **LOGIN**.

3. Select **LICENSING > Citrix Activation System > Activate or Allocate Licenses**.

4. At the **Citrix Activation System** page, enter the customized product license code in the **Your License Code** box and click **Continue**.

5. At the **Citrix Activation System—Attention** page, click **Continue**.

6. At the following page, enter the hostname and the quantity of licenses to allocate and click **Generate**.

NOTE The hostname for the license server is case-sensitive and can be determined by entering **hostname** at a Windows command prompt on the license server machine.

7. At the **Download License File** page, click **Download License File**.

8. At the **File Download** dialog box, click **Save**.

9. At the **Save As** dialog box, specify the download location. Citrix suggests saving these files to a portable storage device. Once the download completes, click **Close**.

10. Back in Internet Explorer, log out by clicking **Logout**.

Protect the License Files

The availability of license files is the most valuable Citrix License Server asset. Protecting these files is important for maintaining the business continuity of any organization that runs Citrix products. License files can become unavailable through the malicious or nonmalicious methods discussed previously.

Secure Access to License Files

Proper ACLs should be used to protect license files locally. By default, the license server files are installed in C:\Program Files\Citrix\Licensing\. The license files are in the **MyFiles** directory. The directory permissions for **MyFiles** should be as follows:

▼ Administrators: Read, Write, and List Folder Contents.

▲ Local system: Read and List Folder Contents. If the License Management Console is used to add licenses, the Local System account needs Write permission as well.

The files within the MyFiles directory need the following permissions:

▼ Citrix.opt

 ■ Administrators need Read and Write permissions.

 ■ Local system needs Read access.

▲ .lic files: Inherit permissions from the parent folder.

Prevent Malicious Checkout of Licenses

An attacker may attempt to check out all the licenses, thus preventing Citrix products and users from utilizing licenses. The license server options file (default C:\Program Files\Citrix\Licensing\MyFiles\CITRIX.opt) allows administrators to specify which servers can check out licenses. This is done through INCLUDE and DENY lists. Servers listed in the INCLUDE list are allowed to request licenses, whereas those in the DENY list are forbidden to do so. The keywords HOST, HOST_GROUP, and INTERNET are valid with INCLUDE and DENY.

▼   HOST: This is the Citrix Access Suite product server name or its IP address. The IP address can contain wildcard characters.

■   HOST_GROUP: This allows administrators to list multiple hosts into a group for easy use in INCLUDE or DENY rules. For more information, see HOST_GROUP in the Citrix Licensing Guide.

▲   INTERNET: This is the Citrix Access Suite product server IP address. The IP address can contain wildcard characters.

The evaluation rules for the INCLUDE and DENY keywords are as follows:

▼   If there is only an INCLUDE list, any host not on that list is denied.

■   If there is only a DENY list, any host not on the list is allowed.

▲   If there are both INCLUDE and DENY lists, the DENY list takes precedence. Any host listed in the DENY list is forbidden even if it is named in the INCLUDE list.

A sample line might look like this:

```
INCLUDE MPS_ENT_CCU HOST toronto

INCLUDE MPS_STD_CCU INTERNET 10.1.123.*
```

The first line allows the host named toronto to use the license MPS_ENT_CCU and by implication prevents all other machines from using that license. The second line allows all hosts within the 10.1.123.0/24 IP block to use the MPS_STD_CCU license, again excluding all other hosts.

To add INCLUDE or DENY lines, administrators need to edit the license server options file (default C:\Program Files\Citrix\Licensing\MyFiles\CITRIX.opt) by using a text editor.

Ensure Business Continuity

To protect against accidental or malicious damage to a license server, administrators should make backups whenever the license files are changed and should back up logs in accordance with the organization's policies. Tapes, images, and swapping hard drives from RAID (Redundant Array of Inexpensive Disks) arrays are all valid methods of defending a license server against damage. To utilize these options, Windows Backup Operator privileges may be required.

Protect the Log Files

The Citrix License Server log files, like all log files, are most valuable when something goes wrong. As an asset, log files have the following threats:

▼   Disclosure

■   Tampering

▲   Destruction

Disclosure of log files may reveal information about an organization such as which Citrix products are being used, the names of licenses, and usage patterns of Citrix products.

> **NOTE**   None of the information contained in the logs is personally identifiable, and no secrets such as usernames or passwords are stored in the log files.

Tampering with log files allows an attacker to conceal his or her activity. Destruction of log files is a significant threat because it eliminates the audit trail completely, though in this case the effect will be very similar to someone tampering with the log files.

Countermeasures

License server log files need to be properly protected to prevent tampering and disclosure of information. The best way to do this is to ensure that only administrators and the logon account used by the CitrixLicensing service have the following access to the log files:

▼   *Administrators*: **Read** access

▲   *The CitrixLicensing service*: **Read** and **Write**

Limiting access to the log files will help prevent disclosure and tampering. To protect logs from tampering or destruction, they should be backed up to another machine or to removable media.

Restrict Access to the License Management Console

The License Management Console is a Web-based management interface to the Citrix License Server. This interface allows an administrator to add or change report logs, generate reports, and upload license files remotely.

User Permissions

The License Management Console allows for a separation of roles between license server users and administrators. This enables individuals to be granted different permissions within the License Management Console based on their assigned roles, as discussed earlier. The credentials of a user who installs the Citrix License Server are set as the default administrator credentials for the License Management Console. This user then can add other users with varying permissions in four categories:

▼   *Current usage*. View which licenses are checked out and aggregate information about license usage.

■   *Historical reporting*. Create reports about license usage. Administrators should protect access to this function to prevent information leakage.

■ *Configuration*. View licenses, force a reload of configuration data, view logs, and configure warnings.

▲ *User administration*. Manage user access to the License Management Console.

To take full advantage of these settings, before installing the License Management Console, it is important to determine which individuals need access to each category. Granting individuals the fewest user permissions they require helps limit the damage that can result from an attacker compromising an individual's account.

NOTE Administrators must ensure that at least one user has full user permissions.

Citrix License Server administrators do not need to be Windows administrators. Taking advantage of this allows a separation of roles. It is necessary for Citrix administrators to have **Read** access to the C:\Program Files\Citrix\Licensing directory. To install or modify license files or the Citrix.opt file, Citrix administrators also need **Write** access to the MyFiles directory.

Remote Access

After determining who needs to access the License Management Console, determine from where those individuals will access it. When allowing remote access, the administrator should protect the network traffic. Administrators are strongly encouraged to set up and configure SSL or TLS on the license server.

Configure License Management Console to Use SSL/TLS   The License Management Console runs as a Web server on port 8080. Microsoft Internet Information Services is used to forward requests locally from port 80 to port 8080. Port 8080 should not be exposed to remote connects. To make License Management Console use SSL/TLS, the administrator must install an SSL certificate and set IIS to use secure communication.

NOTE   This guide covers setting IIS 6.0, the most recent version of IIS as of this writing, to use secure communication. For more information or for administering other versions of IIS, go to http://www.microsoft.com.

NOTE   Setting up SSL/TLS requires an SSL certificate for the server. Administrators can create their own or request one from a third-party certificate authority.

Consult Appendix D, "SSL/TLS Certificate Installation," for information on obtaining and installing digital certificates. The License Management Console should now be accessible only via port 443 by using https://<hostname>/lmc/index.jsp.

NOTE   Administrators will also have to update the Citrix installed shortcuts to the License Management Console to use HTTPS.

Isolate the Citrix License Server behind a Firewall

To further protect the Citrix License Server, it should be segmented away from other networks by using a firewall.

NOTE   Refer to the diagram in the "Components" section for port information and recommended firewall placement.

The Citrix License Server must be specifically configured for firewall support. This requires the following steps:

1. Configure the Citrix Vendor Daemon to use a specified port.
2. Install the firewall.
3. Configure the firewall.

Set Citrix Vendor Daemon Port

Configuring the Citrix Vendor Service requires editing the license files. Administrators must be careful when editing those files. They are very sensitive to change, and modifying anything other than the appropriate lines may render them unusable. Creating a backup copy of the license files before modifying them is highly recommended.

To configure the Citrix Vendor Service to use a static port:

1. Go to **Control Panel > Administrative Tools > Services and Stop the License Management Console for Citrix Licensing Service**.
2. Go to C:\Program Files\Citrix\Licensing\MyFiles, right click on each license file, select **Properties**, and uncheck the **Read-Only** box.
3. Edit each of the license files in a text editor.

NOTE   If any license files are changed, all future license files added to this server must also be edited before they are added to the server.

4. Locate the **VENDOR CITRIX** line and append the following:

```
options=<path to the options file> port=<port number>
```

The following sample configuration line sets the Citrix license daemon to be accessible via TCP port 27950.

```
VENDOR CITRIX options="C:\Program Files\Citrix\Licensing\
MyFiles\CITRIX.opt" port=27950
```

5. Save the license file, ensuring that the .lic file name extension is preserved and that the file is saved in UTF-8 format.
6. To reenable the **Read-Only** attribute on the license file:

   a. Right click on the file.
   b. Select **properties.**
   c. Check the **Read-Only** check box.

NOTE   It is important that the previous steps be completed on all license files before proceeding.

7. Restart the Citrix License Management Console service from the Service Control Manager.
8. Restart the Citrix Licensing service from the Service Control Manager.

To verify the Citrix vendor daemon is properly configured, open the **lmgrd_debug. log** file. This file is located in C:\Program Files\Citrix\Licensing\LS. Look for lines that use the new port number. They will be similar to the following:

```
3:13:48 (lmgrd) lmgrd tcp-port 27000

3:13:51 (lmgrd) CITRIX using port 27950 specified in license file
```

If the Citrix Vendor Service is not using the expected port or if it fails to start, ensure that all the license files were updated to use the correct port. If the Citrix Licensing service detects any discrepancy in the requested ports, it will not start.

Configure Firewall

After verifying that the Citrix vendor daemon has been properly configured, install and configure the firewall.

NOTE   Administrators of organizations that use Citrix Password Manager should be aware that Password Manager Agents (not the Password Manager server) contact the license server. Administrators must set their firewall rules to allow all machines on the trusted intranet that have Password Manager Agent installed to contact the license server.

Configure Auditing

Auditing is an important security tool. Auditing of license checkouts is done through the license server log files. The log files can record checkins, checkouts, and denied checkouts. By default, only denied checkouts are recorded. The logging level is controlled through the NOLOG keyword in the C:\Program Files\Citrix\Licensing\MyFiles\ Citrix.opt file. The NOLOG syntax is as follows:

```
NOLOG {IN | OUT | DENIED}
```

Logging everything provides more information and may help isolate misbehaving hosts, although at the cost of larger logs.

The main threats to both log and configuration files are modification and deletion. The operating system provides mechanisms to track this behavior. To take full advantage of operating system functionality, Windows administrators should be separate individuals from Citrix License Server administrators. This allows an appropriately configured System Access Control List on the Citrix License Server log files to record when the files are modified or deleted. The file system permissions must grant the Citrix administrator at most the following permissions:

▼   Modify

■   Read & Execute

■   Read

▲   Write

Do not grant License Server administrators *Full Control*. This helps preserve the audit trail even if a Citrix License Server administrator's account is compromised, because the Citrix License Server administrator cannot modify the system logs to cover up any misdeeds.

VERIFY THE SECURED CONFIGURATION

To verify that all the security steps have been followed, do the following:

1. From a different machine, run a third-party port scanner and verify that only the expected ports are open.

2. Log in as a Windows nonprivileged user and try to access the license files, the Citrix.opt file, and the log files. This should result in **permission denied** messages.

3. Change the IP address of a Citrix product to one that is not authorized for license checkout and attempt to check out a license. No license should be obtained.

4. Make sure that regular backups are being made.

5. Run the Windows utility `netstat  -ab` and check to see that lmgrd.exe is listening on port 27000 and Citrix.exe is listening on the port specified in the license files.

6. Attempt to log in to the License Management Console as a user who should not have access. This should result in an **access denied** error.

7. Using a third-party network monitor, start a network capture and record as an administrator logs into the License Management Console. Confirm that the traffic is encrypted by SSL/TLS.

SUMMARY

This chapter explored threats to the Citrix License Server, countermeasures to each of those threats, and ways to implement each countermeasure. Always keep the operating system, antivirus software, and license server up to date with the latest security hotfixes and service packs.

APPENDIX A

Other Citrix Solutions

This book discusses the Citrix Presentation Server and Password Manager products. Other Citrix products for access security are described below.

CITRIX ACCESS GATEWAY

Citrix Access Gateway products (Figure A1-1) are universal SSL VPN appliances that provide a secure, always-on single point of access to an organization's applications and data. A comprehensive range of appliances and editions allow Access Gateway to meet the needs of an organization of any size, from small businesses to the most demanding global enterprises.

▼ *Citrix Access Gateway Standard Edition* is easy to deploy, simple to manage, and the most cost-effective secure remote access solution on the market. The Access Gateway appliance is deployed in an organization's DMZ and secures all traffic with standards-based SSL. Remote users connect via an easy-to-use Web-downloaded and -updated client, enjoying a rich desklike experience.

■ *Citrix Access Gateway Advanced Edition* provides access to more devices and users, including browser-only kiosk access and mobile devices. Extensive SmartAccess capabilities provide flexible, highly granular policy-based access control, including the tightest level of integration with the Citrix Presentation Server.

▲ *Citrix Access Gateway Enterprise Edition* is the best solution for demanding enterprise environments, offering maximum scalability, performance, availability, and management. Integrated application acceleration and optimization capabilities increase remote access performance while reducing costs.

Access Gateway delivers the best access experience of any SSL VPN on the market:

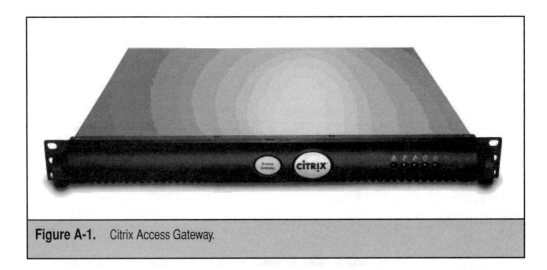

Figure A-1.   Citrix Access Gateway.

▼   *Best user experience.* Access Gateway delivers the same desktop access experience that users have within the network, reducing training and support. In addition, Access Gateway automatically and seamlessly reconnects users to their applications and documents when they change locations and devices, increasing user productivity.

■   *Single point of access.* Access Gateway provides secure access to any application or IT resource, data, and voice, including Windows and UNIX applications, Web applications, Citrix Presentation Server–hosted applications, network file shares, and even telephony services that use VoIP softphones. No application customization or "webification" is required.

■   *Cost-effective.* Access Gateway is fast, easy, and cost-effective to deploy and manage via its Web-deployed autoupdating client and intuitive management tools. Organizations can easily provide their remote users with desklike access from any location without the cost and complexity of installing, configuring, updating, and supporting client software on each device.

▲   *Strengthened data security.* Access Gateway offers a range of secure hardened appliances, all with standards-based SSL/TLS encryption and extensive authentication support, including two-factor authentication tokens and smart cards. Integrated endpoint scanning ensures that a device is safe to connect to the network.

The Only SmartAccess SSL VPN

Citrix Access Gateway is the only SSL VPN with *SmartAccess* capabilities: highly granular policy-based access with sense-and-respond technology. SmartAccess improves productivity without compromising security by analyzing the access scenario and delivering the appropriate level of access, including control of actions such as print, save, and edit.

With Citrix SmartAccess, access becomes like a dimmer switch in which the right level of access can be dialed and configured for any access scenario. Other SSL VPNs can provide only an "on/off" access capability.

The Best SSL VPN to Use with Citrix Presentation Server

Citrix Access Gateway can be deployed with or without a Citrix Presentation Server. When deployed with a Citrix Presentation Server, Access Gateway can be configured to emulate the secure gateway feature, allowing direct connection from Citrix Presentation Server (ICA) clients. Using Access Gateway with Citrix Presentation Server delivers the benefits of a hardened appliance-based universal SSL VPN, increasing security, extending user access, and reducing costs.

The Best Remote Access Solution

Citrix Access Gateway is the best remote access solution from the most trusted name in secure on-demand access. No other SSL VPN offers such an efficient cost-effective remote access experience. For more information, go to http://www.citrix/com/accessgateway.

CITRIX APPLICATION FIREWALL

Citrix Application Firewall is a high-performance hardened security appliance that blocks all known and unknown attacks against Web and Web Services applications. Citrix Application Firewall enforces a positive security model that permits only correct application behavior without relying on attack signatures. Application Firewall analyzes all bidirectional traffic, including SSL-encrypted communications, protecting against 16 classes of Web application vulnerabilities without any modification to applications.

Citrix Application Firewall is available as a family of purpose-built appliances that meet any deployment need and comes in two software editions that offer upgrade options as threats, applications, and defenses become more complex. Application Firewall is deployable stand-alone or in concert with Citrix NetScaler Application Delivery systems to deliver the combined benefits of application optimization and comprehensive protection.

▼ *Citrix Application Firewall Standard Edition* offers full protection against the most common and dangerous Web application threats, high-performance security for both Web and XML Web Services applications, and full protection against data theft. It can be seamlessly upgraded to the Enterprise Edition.

▲ *Citrix Application Firewall Enterprise Edition* adds advanced learning capabilities to protect against more sophisticated application attacks, provides protection against attacks that target specific user sessions (mandatory for e-commerce and secure extranet and online banking applications), and provides more granular control over application security policies.

Citrix Application Firewall is available on multiple hardware platforms to meet the performance and availability requirements of any organization from small enterprises to large data centers. FIPS-140-2 Level 3-compliant models are also available.

Addressing Today's Security Challenges

Network-level security infrastructures such as firewalls and intrusion prevention systems cannot defend against application layer attacks, leaving applications and servers exposed to a myriad of known and unknown exploits. Application Firewall comprehensively addresses the challenge of delivering centralized application layer security for all Web and Web Services applications.

The Positive Security Model Advantage

Citrix Application Firewall enforces a positive security model to ensure correct application behavior. Instead of relying on attack signatures or pattern-matching techniques, the positive security model understands "good" application behavior and blocks as malicious any deviation from proper application activities. It is the only proven approach that delivers "zero-day" protection against unpublished exploits.

Powerful Business Object Protection

Citrix Application Firewall prevents in real time the inadvertent disclosure of sensitive application content, which could result in identity theft and fraud. Business object protection modules help secure both predefined objects such as U.S. Social Security numbers or credit card numbers and administratively defined data objects. By detecting erroneous disclosures and blocking or rewriting content, business object protection modules help to conform to governmental privacy regulations.

Centralized Security for All Web and Web Services Applications

Application Firewall can secure an organization's entire Web and Web services applications infrastructure, with complete administrative separation of application security policies, controls, reporting details, and log data.

The Best Application Security Solution

Citrix Application Firewall is the best Web application and Web services security solution; no other application firewall offers such an efficient cost-effective remote access experience. For more information, go to http://www.citrix.com/applicationfirewall.

CITRIX NETSCALER APPLICATION DELIVERY

Citrix NetScaler Application Delivery systems accelerate the performance of applications by up to 15 times while providing comprehensive L4-7 traffic management, server offload capabilities, and essential application protection. The NetScaler Application Delivery product line consists of the Citrix NetScaler Application Switch and Citrix NetScaler Application Accelerator solutions.

Citrix NetScaler Application Switch is a high-performance application delivery system that accelerates applications by up to 15 times. The Enterprise Edition enhances application infrastructure by providing comprehensive traffic management, application acceleration and availability, network optimization, and defenses against attacks. The Citrix NetScaler Application Switch is available in Standard Edition and Enterprise Edition.

Accelerated Application Performance

▼ Lowers application response times with data compression for HTTP and all TCP-based traffic.

■ Optimizes the application delivery infrastructure with multiple TCP optimizations.

▲ Integrates ASIC-based SSL acceleration for faster delivery of secure Web traffic (HTTPS).

Load Balancing and Content Switching

▼   Intelligently distributes application requests based on layer 4 or layer 7 information.

■   Reduces application response times and optimizes server infrastructures.

■   Delivers robust high availability for any application infrastructure.

▲   Provides global traffic management for multisite enterprises via global load balancing and disaster recovery.

Application Security

▼   Protects application availability with defenses against denial-of-service (DoS) attacks.

▲   Blocks Web-based worms and application attacks with intrusion protection features.

Citrix NetScaler Application Accelerator is a high-performance application delivery system that accelerates applications by up to 15 times, assures performance for legitimate clients while defending against denial-of-service attacks, and delivers secure remote access. NetScaler Application Accelerator can be deployed stand-alone or augment existing layer 4 to layer 7 load-balancing systems.

NetScaler Application Accelerator is powered by the NetScaler Operating System, a purpose-build modular operating system that delivers industry-leading performance to small and large enterprise deployments.

Accelerates Application Performance

▼   Optimizes the application delivery infrastructure with multiple TCP optimizations.

■   Accelerates delivery of Web and client-server application data with compression for HTTP- and TCP-based traffic.

■   Enhances application performance while lowering server workload with static and dynamic content caching.

▲   Accelerates secure Web application delivery with SSL offload.

Delivers End-to-End Secure Access

▼   High-performance content encryption for HTTPS

▲   Secure remote access to all TCP-based applications with SSL VPN

Defends Against Denial-of-Service Attacks

▼ Protects application servers from denial-of-service attacks.

▲ Ensures uninterrupted access for legitimate traffic during malicious attacks.

The Best Web Application Delivery Solution

Citrix Netscaler Application Accelerator is the Web application delivery solution. No other form of application delivery offers such efficient cost-effective acceleration, traffic management, and attack protection. For more information, go to http://www.citrix.com/netscaler.

APPENDIX B

Checklists

SECURE GATEWAY

The following steps should be taken to secure the Secure Gateway.

Check	Description
❏	Secure the operating system
❏	Install the Secure Gateway as a nonprivileged user
❏	Configure the Secure Gateway Configuration Wizard
❏	Restrict access to the Secure Gateway
❏	Enable IPsec between the Secure Gateway and the Presentation Server
❏	Protect the log files
❏	Configure auditing
❏	Verify the secured configuration

WEB INTERFACE

The following steps should be taken to secure the Web Interface.

Check	Description
❏	Secure the operating system
❏	Restrict access to the Web Interface server
❏	Configure authentication
❏	Secure the link between the Web Interface and the Presentation Server
❏	Secure the link between the Web Interface and the Secure Gateway
❏	Secure the Web Interface for use with the Program Neighborhood Agent
❏	Protect log files
❏	Configure auditing
❏	Verify the secured configuration

PASSWORD MANAGER AGENT

The following steps should be taken to secure the Password Manager Agent.

Check	Description
❏	Configure the Password Manager Agent with smart cards
❏	Create a secure user configuration
❏	Configure the secure user configuration
❏	Create a secure password policy
❏	Verify the secured configuration

PASSWORD MANAGER SERVICE

The following steps should be taken to secure the Password Manager Service.

Check	Description
❏	Secure the operating system by using the Security Configuration Wizard
❏	Enable the Data Integrity Module
❏	Configure auditing
❏	Secure the Password Manager Service data
❏	Verify the secured configuration

PASSWORD MANAGER CENTRAL STORE

The following steps should be taken to secure the Password Manager Central Store.

Check	Description
❏	Secure the operating system by using the Security Configuration Wizard
❏	Secure an NTFS network share central store
❏	Secure the Active Directory container central store
❏	Verify the secured configuration

PRESENTATION SERVER

The following steps should be taken to secure the Presentation Server.

Check	Description
❏	Secure the operating system
❏	Configure authentication
❏	Configure secure communications
❏	Configure client drive mapping
❏	Configure client clipboard mapping
❏	Configure client device mapping
❏	Secure the IMA data store
❏	Configure Citrix Administrator accounts
❏	Configure Citrix Connection Configuration
❏	Configure Terminal Services Configuration
❏	Configure Presentation Server policies
❏	Configure Group Policy for the Presentation Server
❏	Secure the SNMP configuration
❏	Secure IMA communication
❏	Access the Presentation Server Console only as a published application
❏	Access the Access Suite Console only as a published application
❏	Secure printer connections
❏	Secure Installation Manager deployments
❏	Secure the Citrix XML Service and Secure Ticket Authority
❏	Only launch published applications
❏	Secure the Pass-Through Client
❏	Run published applications only as a nonprivileged user
❏	Remove Remote Desktop Protocol access
❏	Disable administrative shares
❏	Configure auditing
❏	Verify the secured configuration

PRESENTATION SERVER CLIENT

The following steps should be taken to secure the Presentation Server Client.

Check	Description
❏	Configure authentication
❏	Configure secure communications
❏	Run the client only as a nonprivileged user
❏	Disable client drive mapping
❏	Disable undesired device mappings
❏	Disable the bitmap disk cache
❏	Verify the secured configuration

LICENSE SERVER

The following steps should be taken to secure the License Server.

Check	Description
❏	Secure the operating system
❏	Download the license files
❏	Protect the license files
❏	Protect the log files
❏	Restrict access to the License Management Console
❏	Isolate the Citrix License Server behind a firewall
❏	Configure auditing
❏	Verify the secured configuration

APPENDIX C

Additional Resources

The links listed below are to additional security resources on the World Wide Web.

Citrix

▼ Citrix Resource Site

http://www.citrix.com/security

■ Citrix Service Packs, Patches, and Components Download

http://www.citrix.com/lang/English/downloads.asp

■ Citrix Systems Support

http://www.citrix.com/lang/English/support.asp

■ Citrix Knowledge Center

http://support.citrix.com/

■ Citrix Security Bulletins

http://support.citrix.com/latestsecurityall!execute.jspa

■ Citrix Common Criteria

http://www.citrix.com/English/aboutCitrix/legal/secondLevel
.asp?level2ID=13437

■ Citrix Security Standards (including FIPS)

http://www.citrix.com/English/aboutCitrix/legal/secondLevel
.asp?level2ID=5405

■ Citrix Affiliations in Security Groups

http://www.citrix.com/site/jumpPage.asp?pageID=22213

■ Citrix Password Manager Authentication Partners

http://www.citrix.com/English/ps2/products/feature.asp?contentID=21009

▲ Citrix Password Manager Security Assessment

http://www.citrix.com/English/ps2/products/feature.asp?contentID=21006

Windows

▼ Microsoft Security

http://www.microsoft.com/security/

■ Security updates from Microsoft

http://www.microsoft.com/athome/security/update/bulletins/default.mspx

■ Securing Data in Transit with IPsec

http://www.windowsecurity.com/articles/Securing_Data_in_Transit_with_IPSec
.html

■ Microsoft NTLM

http://msdn.microsoft.com/library/default.asp?url=/library/en-us/secauthn/
security/microsoft_ntlm.asp

■ NTLM Authentication

http://msdn.microsoft.com/library/default.asp?url=/library/en-us/rtcclnt/rtc/
ntlm_authentication.asp

■ Group Policy page

http://www.microsoft.com/technet/grouppolicy

▲ Active Directory page

http://www.microsoft.com/windowsserver2003/technologies/directory/
activedirectory/default.mspx

Security

▼ Computer Emergency Response Team (CERT)

http://www.cert.org/

■ Computer Security Resource Center

http://csrc.nist.gov/

▲ SANS Institute

http://www.sans.org/

Standards and Compliance

▼ Common Criteria Portal

http://www.commoncriteriaportal.org/

■ FIPS 140-2 information

http://csrc.nist.gov/cryptval/140-2.htm

■ Full text of FIPS 140-2

http://csrc.nist.gov/publications/fips/fips140-2/fips1402.pdf

■ Netscape's SSL 3.0 specification

http://wp.netscape.com/eng/ssl3/draft302.txt

■ The IETF TLS Working Group

http://www.ietf.org/html.charters/tls-charter.html

■ TLS 1.1

http://tools.ietf.org/html/4346

- HTTP Over TLS
  http://tools.ietf.org/html/2818
- TLS Extensions
  http://tools.ietf.org/html/4366
- IPsec IETF charter
  http://www.ietf.org/html.charters/OLD/ipsec-charter.html
- IPsec protocols
  http://tools.ietf.org/html/2401
  http://tools.ietf.org/html/2402
  http://tools.ietf.org/html/2403
  http://tools.ietf.org/html/2404
  http://tools.ietf.org/html/2405
  http://tools.ietf.org/html/2406
  http://tools.ietf.org/html/2407
  http://tools.ietf.org/html/2408
  http://tools.ietf.org/html/2409
  http://tools.ietf.org/html/2410
  http://tools.ietf.org/html/2411
  http://tools.ietf.org/html/2412
  http://tools.ietf.org/html/4301
  http://tools.ietf.org/html/4302
  http://tools.ietf.org/html/4303
  http://tools.ietf.org/html/4304
  http://tools.ietf.org/html/4305
  http://tools.ietf.org/html/4306
  http://tools.ietf.org/html/4307
  http://tools.ietf.org/html/4308
  http://tools.ietf.org/html/4309
- Kerberos Page at MIT
  http://web.mit.edu/kerberos/
- Kerberos v5
  http://tools.ietf.org/html/4120

- HTTP/1.1 RFC

  http://tools.ietf.org/html/2616

- Common Internet File System (CIFS) File Access Protocol

  http://www.microsoft.com/downloads/details.aspx?FamilyID=c4adb584-7ff0-4acf-bd91-5f7708adb23c&displaylang=en

- XML 1.1 Specification

  http://www.w3.org/TR/xml11

- Annotated XML Specification

  http://www.xml.com/axml/testaxml.htm

- XML-DEV Mailing List

  http://www.xml-dev.com:7070/list/xmldev.en.html

- ▲ Internet Control Message Protocol (ICMP) RFC

  http://tools.ietf.org/html/792

Reporting Security Vulnerabilities to Citrix

Citrix welcomes input about the security of its products and takes any and all potential vulnerabilities very seriously. If you would like to report a security issue to Citrix, send an e-mail to secure@citrix.com containing the exact version of the product in which the vulnerability was found and the steps taken to reproduce the vulnerability.

APPENDIX D

SSL/TLS Certificate Installation

WINDOWS

Requesting a Certificate

A certificate signing request (CSR) must be submitted to a Certificate Authority (CA). The Certificate Authority in turn will return the signed SSL/TLS certificate and password. An organization's own procedures for obtaining signed certificates should be followed.

> **NOTE** The common name field in the certificate must be the fully qualified domain name of the server.

The Microsoft Web Server Certificate Wizard in the Internet Information Services snap-in can be used to request and import a server certificate. The wizard can be used to request a certificate signing request from an external CA or request and install the certificate from an internal CA.

To Request a Certificate by Using IIS

1. Click **Start > Programs > Administrative Tools > Internet Services Manager**.

2. In the **Internet Information Services Console** tree, select the **Default Web Site** node and choose **Properties** from the **Action** menu.

3. Navigate to the **Directory Security** tab and select **Server Certificate**. The **IIS Web Server Certificate** wizard appears.

4. Click **Next**.

5. Select **Create a New Certificate** and then click **Next**.

6. Select **Prepare the request now, but send it later** and then click **Next**.

7. In the **Name** field, type the name for the server certificate. The **Name** field is not required to be the FQDN of the server; it can be the server name.

8. In the **Bit Length** field, enter the bit length to be used for the certificate's encryption strength. The greater the bit length, the higher the level of security. If specifying a bit length higher than 1024, verify that the client connecting to the server can support it. Click **Next**.

9. Enter details about the organization. Click **Next**.

10. In **Common Name**, type the FQDN of the server. Click **Next**.

11. Fill in the relevant geographical information. Click **Next**.

12. Save the certificate request and click **Next**. Verify the information in the **Request File Summary**.

13. Click **Next** and then click **Finish**.

The information in the request can be sent to any CA for signing.

Installing the Certificate by Using Microsoft Management Console

1. Launch the Microsoft Management Console by choosing **Start > Run** and then typing **mmc**. Click **OK**.

2. If **Certificates** is not listed in the **Console Root** folder, the **Certificates** snap-in must be added.

   ■ From the console menu, choose **Add/Remove Snap-in**. The **Add/Remove Snap-in** dialog box appears.

   ■ Click **Add**. The **Add Standalone Snap-in** dialog box appears.

   ■ Select **Certificates** and click **Add**. The **Certificates snap-in** dialog box appears.

   ■ Click **Computer account** and then click **Next**. The **Select Computer** dialog box appears.

   ■ Verify that **Local computer** is selected and then click **Finish**.

   ■ Click **Close** to close the **Add Standalone Snap-in** dialog box.

   ■ Click **OK** to close the **Add/Remove Snap-in** dialog box.

3. In the left pane of the console, click the plus sign (+) for **Certificates (Local Computer)** to expand the folder.

4. Click the plus sign (+) to expand the **Personal** folder and then click **Certificates**.

5. In the right pane, select the certificate to import.

6. From the **Action** menu, select **All Tasks** and then click **Import**. The Certificate Import wizard appears.

7. Click **Next** and then click **Browse** to search for the certificate file to be imported.

8. Select the certificate file and click **Next**.

9. Enter the private key password in the **Password** box and click **Next**.

10. Click **Next** to accept the default values in the next window and then click **Finish** to import the certificate.

UNIX/LINUX

To enable SSL/TLS on Tomcat, follow these steps:

1. Generate a keypair and a CSR with the Java keytool:

```
keytool -certreq -genkey -alias tomcat -keyalg RSA -file
server.csr
```

2. Modify the default keystore and alias passwords for Apache/Tomcat by editing conf/server.xml in the Tomcat installation directory.

3. Submit the CSR (server.csr) to a CA.

4. After receiving the signed certificate, convert the certificate into the format required by Java (Tomcat):

```
keytool -import -alias tomcat -file server.der
```

5. Edit conf/servers.xml. Locate the SSL HTTP/1.1 connection. Set the port to the well-known SSL port 443.

6. Restart Tomcat.

7. Navigate to "https://server/Citrix/" and log in. Launch a published application.

INDEX

B

R

 S

T

U

X